PRAISE FOR *E.......* ......

"This book is a powerful guide for navigating the journey to self-love and discovering the master within you. One of the most valuable things about *Energy Speaks* is that Lee Harris and the Zs give us easy processes to cultivate personal happiness, inner peace, and well-being. No matter where you are in your life, this book can offer you an exercise, affirmation, or pearl of wisdom that can make your life better today. Buy this book and, more importantly, read it!"

— **Sara Landon,** globally celebrated transformational leader, speaker, and channeler

"On a personal level, shedding the spiritual, emotional, and mental toxicity with Lee Harris and the Zs made me a much lighter, happier, more compassionate, more connected person, not to mention a far better wife, mother, and friend. On a professional level, it put me into the flow of great new opportunities and creative ideas."

— **Natalia Rose,** author of nine books, including *The Raw Food Detox Diet*, and founder of Natalia Rose Institute

"Lee Harris and the Zs have the extraordinary ability to communicate complex spiritual concepts in a loving and concise way. The powerful exercises in *Energy Speaks* have the potential to radically transform the reader's life. A must-read for anyone seeking to become more intuitive, heart-centered, and self-aware!"

— **Wendy Kennedy,** channeler, speaker, and coauthor of *The Great Human Potential* (www.HigherFrequencies.net)

"I have been blessed to listen to, come to know, and interview many. There are but two that carry a frequency that stands out among the many, and Lee Harris is one for sure. Adding to that is his beautiful heart that stands behind his every word and carries great impact."

— **Maureen Moss,** author, president of
the New World Puja Network, and radio host of *Thrive*

"Lee Harris is a channel and spiritual teacher with an international following. *Energy Speaks*, a distillation of teachings on subjects ranging from abundance to sleep to sexuality, is a gentle and openhearted offering as Lee supports his readers in claiming a higher and more authentic expression of their lives."

— **Paul Selig,** channel and author of *The Book of Freedom*

"Lee Harris may be the most insightful, authentic, and caring energy empath I have met in a lifetime of seeking."

— **Mike Dooley,** *New York Times* bestselling author of
Infinite Possibilities

"Lee Harris is a rock-star medium. His insights are spot-on, his delivery real and accessible. *Energy Speaks*, a profound manifesto for personal power, acts like rocket fuel for those of us who want to live more consciously and love more courageously. This is exactly the book our world needs right now — one you'll return to many times, and one that will energize and inspire you with each reading."

— **Scott Stabile,** author of *Big Love:
The Power of Living with a Wide-Open Heart*

ENERGY
SPEAKS

ENERGY SPEAKS

Messages from Spirit on
**LIVING, LOVING,
and AWAKENING**

LEE HARRIS

Foreword by Regina Meredith

New World Library
Novato, California

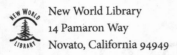 New World Library
14 Pamaron Way
Novato, California 94949

Text design by Tona Pearce Myers

Library of Congress Cataloging-in-Publication Data

Names: Harris, Lee, 1976- author.
Title: Energy speaks : messages from spirit on living, loving, and awakening / Lee Harris.
Description: Novato : New World Library, 2019.
Identifiers: LCCN 2018046649 (print) | LCCN 2019009458 (ebook) | ISBN 9781608685967 (ebook) | ISBN 9781608685950 (print : alk. paper)
Subjects: LCSH: Spirit writings. | Channeling (Spiritualism)
Classification: LCC BF1290 (ebook) | LCC BF1290 .H37 2019 (print) | DDC 133.9/3--dc23
LC record available at https://lccn.loc.gov/2018046649

First printing, March 2019
ISBN 978-1-60868-595-0
Ebook ISBN 978-1-60868-596-7
Printed in Canada on 100% postconsumer-waste recycled paper

 New World Library is proud to be a Gold Certified Environmentally Responsible Publisher. Publisher certification awarded by Green Press Initiative.

10   9   8   7   6

This book is dedicated to all the students, private session clients, and workshop participants I have met through this work.
You taught me how to do this job.
Thank you for letting me listen to you.
Thank you for letting the Zs and me speak.
Thank you for changing my life.
With love and deep gratitude to all of you.

CONTENTS

Foreword by Regina Meredith   xiii
Introduction: When Destiny Calls   1

Chapter 1. You Are a Lightworker: Owning Your Personal Power   20

Exercise: Connecting with Your Soul Power   25
Exercise: Identifying Your Soul Group   27
Closing Exercise with Lee: Calling Back Your Power   32
The Lightworker Affirmation   33

Chapter 2. Your Self-Love Journey   34

Opening Relaxation Exercise   35
Energy Meditation: The 5-Minute Flame   47
Sacred Commitment Ceremony   53
Self-Love Energy Exercise and Affirmations   54

Chapter 3. The Art of Receiving   55

Exercise: Releasing Guilt   57
Exercise: Opening to Options and Possibilities   59
The Receiving Affirmation   69

Chapter 4. Abundance   70

Visionary Exercise: Abundant You   75
Meditation: Abundance = Wholeheartedness   79
Abundance Exercise and Affirmation   82

Chapter 5. Loving Money   85

Inquiry Exercise: How Much Money Are You Ready For?   91
Exercise of Breath and Light: Loving Money   95
Visualization: Walking Your Money Path   97
The Money Affirmation   102

Chapter 6. Sleep: A Surprising Key to Self-Mastery   103

Exercise: Requesting an Energetic Shift   108
The Sleep Affirmation   113

Chapter 7. The Eye of Awareness   114

Visualization: Activating the Eye of Awareness   117
The Awareness Affirmation   128

Chapter 8. Sex and Sexual Energy   129

Awareness Exercise: Uncovering Sexual Beliefs   132
The Sacred Fire Affirmation   140

Chapter 9. The Essence of Successful Relationships:
Tapping Into the Energy of Trust   141

Exercise: Connecting Energetically to the Heart
  of a Lost Love   146
Exercise: Entering into Love's Healing Zone   155
Exercise: Seeing the Real You   158
The Relationship Affirmation   160

Chapter 10. Family Peace   161

Exercise: Dissolving Family Energy Blocks   169
Family Freedom Exercise and Affirmation   176

Chapter 11. The Power of Women   177

Exercise: Opening Your Heart to Your Mother and Father   185
The Feminine Energy Affirmation   191

Chapter 12. Radical Expression: The Doorway to Transformation   192

Writing Exercise for Transformation:
    Radical Expression in Action   208

Chapter 13. The Angel Behind You   211

Visualization: Wrapped in Angel Wings   220
Held in the Light Affirmation   223

Closing: You Are Love   224

Acknowledgments   229
Lee Harris Energy Resources   231
About the Author   233

FOREWORD

L ee Harris and his guides, the Zs, speak for a new generation of
spiritual seekers — those who know they have been told half-
truths and want to find meaning and depth in their lives. *Energy
Speaks* is an answer to this need.

We are living in times when the spirit is drawing closer to our
conscious awareness, which is a both beautiful and confusing part
of our evolution. As we begin to sense a larger array of emotions,
this information can clash with the agendas being played out by
our thoughts. *Energy Speaks* serves as a guide to begin connecting
deeply with these feelings.

In his young life, as with many in the younger generations,
Lee's feelings came in perpendicular to his thoughts. This can
create a kind of cognitive dissonance, leaving a person to doubt
themselves. This confusion dominated Lee's early years, with the
perpetual question "Which are true: my thoughts or my feelings?"
He was given divine intervention to begin answering that question and shares that journey with the reader of this book. For the

rest of us, now is a perfect time to be asking that question and "listening" to the answers.

As humanity moves into this more fluid state of feeling, we begin to notice that we are moving closer to our true nature. Try as we might to push these feelings down, they seem to be uncannily correct in what they are showing us. Why? Because these higher feelings are being informed by our Higher Mind. This is not true of lower-mind emotions, which are subconsciously programmed to inform us of the world surrounding us. *Energy Speaks* shows us that if we ignore either, it will be at our own expense.

Our emotional baggage is giving us a glimpse into all that has come before this moment, all of it recorded in our energy field called the *aura*. We encounter a certain scent, scene, person, food, or activity and we respond viscerally — the result of a previous experience that has become imprinted upon our subconscious. In the best sense, this serves as a guidance system, warning us away from something that has caused pain, confusion, or loss at another time in our deep past. Conversely, this very same stimulus can cause us to run away from opportunity because we have had an unfortunate experience with it in the past. The more we dial into our higher feelings, however, the more we begin to discern the difference between the more sublime providence of those feelings and the denser demands of the emotions. This helps us decide wisely when it is time to engage or flee. It is ultimately our choice.

In *Energy Speaks* there is a great emphasis on choice, from the choice of our parents prior to birth, to the planet on which we elect to be born, and even our surrounding support group. This includes the unseen realms of beings who are here to assist us in reaching our souls' desired goals or lessons for a given lifetime. The messages of this book contain wisdom from Lee's guides, who not only have helped him work through the challenging moments of his life but have worked *through* him to help all of humanity. Lee has agreed to this arrangement, which is explained in this book.

In my life, I, too, listen to guides, even when the messages are not comfortable. A chronicle of some of these messages and events is narrated in my book *Accidentally on Purpose: Tripping through Life with Regina*. These wise messages from realms beyond challenge our existing beliefs and paradigms and yet are validated well when we listen to them. Otherwise we would simply tell ourselves stories we like to hear to reinforce our existing reality. As Lee says in this book, guides have no problem telling you that you are flat-out wrong if they have to!

For Lee, some of these messages address the subject of the masculine and feminine, as well as sexuality. The Zs speak directly to these delicate and powerful aspects of our human nature, and one message comes through very clearly in this book: the time of the feminine has arrived.

Why the feminine?

The feminine is the creative aspect of our true self — all of us, both men and women. Our creativity is born of our ability to listen to the Higher Mind and our guides. Our Higher Mind and guides are constantly standing by, whispering the desire of the soul into our hearts, inviting it to express itself. In fact, the Zs insist that when we ignore these creative impulses, we can diminish the quality of our lives to the point of depression. This is the reflection of a withering spirit, a soul that is not being heard.

Because the feminine is receptive in nature, she has a greater ability to listen to the higher voice perpetually whispering its guidance to us. This also puts us in closer contact with our emotions. *Energy Speaks* insists that until we all listen to these emotions, giving them respect, we cannot unblock the pathways to our full creative expression on Earth — and this potential is vast!

On the challenging side of the feminine, competition between women is still holding back the progression of consciousness among us. Emerging from darker times of patriarchy, in which women felt a need to compete for mere survival, old patterns die hard. The Zs speak about the need for women to begin relaxing into our own empowered voice, which is fueled by the activeness of the masculine. Until we master this, we remain attached to subconscious reactions prompted by our past circumstances.

It is the responsibility of the new man to honor and express his emotions and feelings in order to bring *his* genius to light. It is the responsibility of the new woman to utter her truth in a powerful way in order to bring *her* genius to light. The meeting of these two creates worlds of new possibility for confronting the challenges of life on Earth. What a beautiful progression from where we stand now!

Lee and the Zs insist that the human species is rich and complex as a direct result of having such strong emotions and feelings. From them come our gifts and talents and our true power. *Energy Speaks* details what this power is — an ability to listen to our higher truth and actively choose to *live into* it. This is the great promise of the times: for each of us to live into our divine genius by engaging, in the deepest sense, with our emotions, mind, and spirit. This book serves as a gateway to defining what this journey requires from each and every one of us. I invite you to enjoy the ride!

Regina Meredith,
journalist and host of Gaia TV's *Open Minds*
(www.ReginaMeredith.com)

INTRODUCTION

WHEN DESTINY CALLS

───❦───

In the year 2000, when I was twenty-three years old, my life changed forever.

I was gliding along on the London Underground train one morning on my way to my job in fund-raising. I was sifting through my thoughts, as I did every morning. As was often the case, I would find many of my thoughts that day to be difficult ones. It was my standard operating procedure back then to take inventory of the things I wasn't happy about and didn't think were going very well, doubling down on the belief that I wasn't good enough. Years of inner torment as a teenager still lingered, plaguing my internal dialogue with self-doubt, self-judgment, and self-blame.

I was thinking about a conflict I was having in my relationship at that time — still bristling from the night before and certain of my position — when a voice stopped me in my tracks.

"That's an interesting perspective, but you're wrong," the voice said.

It wasn't a voice I had heard before, and it wasn't coming from me. If I had to describe it in practical terms, it was as if the voice was coming from about ten inches above my head and to the left. It was loving but firm and instantly shifted my attention away from the negative self-talk I had running in my head.

All this came as a shock. I hadn't been praying or meditating or doing an affirmation exercise. I wasn't asking for guidance. I was just minding my own business, racking my brain over what wasn't working in my life.

I asked this very assertive presence if it had a name. The response further surprised me.

"We don't really have names, but we know that names are useful to you. I'm Zachary, the lead spokesperson for your team of guides. We are eighty-eight entities, but then we extend wider into source."

This was my formal introduction to the Zs, as I have come to call them.

During the first few years after this first blind date with spirit, two additional guides identified themselves — Zapharia and Ziadora — making it a trio of spokespeople. Unlike Zachary, it was explained to me, Zapharia and Ziadora held more feminine energy. The three of them would take turns speaking based on the topic at hand, balancing masculine and feminine energies and perspectives.

By 2013, the Zs had told me that it was no longer necessary for them to communicate in this differentiated way. They said that while it had been useful in the early years for the people who were first encountering my work to separate out the feminine and the masculine, an integrated voice had now become more useful and relevant.

The arrival of the Zs, although wildly unexpected on one level, had been preceded by several years of spiritual seeking. As a teenager, I sought answers to my emotional pain and solace from a world in which I often felt like a stranger. Like many people who identify with being sensitive, empathic, or spiritual, I felt like an outsider most of the time.

Now I understand that all of us, at one time or another, feel like outsiders. When we're going through big change or deep loss, there can be a crisis of identity. We lose a job, a home, or a relationship, or we go through an illness or another dark night of the soul, and suddenly we may feel alien, like strangers to ourselves.

The Zs, as you will discover in this book, are steadfast in their message that we as human beings are never truly alone and never really outsiders. Each one of us is an irreplaceable part of something greater than we can imagine. There is a profound purpose to every one of our lives — even when we have lost the thread of that truth.

I know firsthand what it's like to feel deeply conflicted about my emotions, myself, and life, which is how that auspicious morning on the Tube train happened in the first place.

I had a real dichotomy going on as a child. While I was passionately involved in theater from the age of nine until I was nineteen, when it came to emotions and feelings, I was stifled. I was a creative, highly sensitive kid. Yet it was difficult for me to express emotion or to be around people who couldn't express themselves emotionally. And why that was important to me is because I was actually very emotional. But instead of seeing that as just who I was, with a smidge of neutrality, I saw it as a really big problem. I was absolutely convinced that being so emotional was a major problem for me and for others around me.

For example, I would get upset about things like field day at my school. I was an overweight kid and would feel panicked at the idea of having to compete in running races and other competitive sports. It would cause me anxiety for days beforehand. I would plead with my parents to write me a note to get out of the whole nightmare. Of course, they didn't, and they were right not to. They understood that I needed to learn to do these things. But I felt very humiliated.

Even though I was raised in a loving, normal family, I felt a lot of shame as a child, and at the time I associated it almost entirely with my weight. I developed a food addiction, overeating sugary foods in an attempt to comfort myself. You know you may have a problem when your parents are taking you to Weight Watchers at the ripe old age of ten!

Being overweight so young was deeply painful and really left its mark on me. Other kids regularly verbally bullied me because of my size. Luckily, I was never physically bullied, but I remember certain kids and adults looking at me with what felt like disgust. As a boy, I was good at reading the energy going on around me. I may not have been correctly interpreting every situation, but I noticed the subtle changes in people. I noticed if somebody looked me up and down, forming an opinion about me because of the way I looked, and sometimes dismissing me.

Each of these moments burrowed deeply into my psyche, and while in my mind I assigned my overwhelming shame to the way my body looked, the truth is that the wound was much bigger than that.

I identified as being gay early on in life. Realizing that I was attracted to the same sex rather than the opposite sex felt like a nightmare to me. I remember a period of time between the ages of eleven and twelve when every night for months I secretly prayed that my homosexuality would be taken away — hoping that I would wake up and by some miracle be a person who could just fit in with the rest of society.

Back then I didn't know any gay people, and we certainly didn't have awareness of LGBTQ rights the way they exist now. Teenagers today are growing up in a world that is more accepting of being gay or transgender. But in the late eighties, many still feared and mocked gay people.

There was a very popular UK soap called *EastEnders* that ran on the BBC starting in the mid-eighties. When I was around eleven, a gay kiss on one of the episodes caused a huge furor. In my very early, unformed thoughts, the controversy around it solidified a belief that what I was feeling was wrong. That inevitably translated in my young psyche into a belief that *who I was*, in essence, was wrong.

Luckily, the power of television can run both ways.

I remember seeing *The Oprah Winfrey Show* for the first time when I was sixteen. This was in the early days, before Oprah began having self-help authors and spiritual teachers on the show. She mostly had everyday folk on, talking about their struggles and how they overcame them. Perhaps most significantly, they talked about how they were *feeling*. I had never seen such emotional honesty in my life. I was immediately hooked, and this show became my daily oxygen. It was so liberating to hear people speaking honestly about their circumstances and emotions — not just the good stuff but also the very tough stuff.

Watching Oprah's show helped me see and understand myself in a new light because it showed real, multifaceted people who felt their feelings, people who sometimes cried and found ways out of their pain. It was a forum that invited and welcomed authenticity rather than settling for masks of politeness and acceptability. This may have had a particular poignancy for me because I was growing up in England thirty years ago, when repression and suppression were more ingrained in our culture than they are today.

My liberation continued as I started to tell close friends that I was gay. They were so cool with it. Again, I felt like I could *breathe*. That time of coming out is when I began to liberate my body as well as my voice, and I started to lose weight. I was 5′8″ at the time, a smaller frame than now, and weighed 15.5 stone, which is about 217 pounds. Over the next two years, I grew to 5′11″ while also losing over sixty pounds.

Theater continued to be a central part of my life at this same time. Because I was struggling to express myself as a person, to be fully expressed as someone else was very freeing. Theater work can be deeply revelatory, like a shamanic act of transformation. For example, if you play a repressed person, you learn something about the repressed part of yourself that you bring forward to connect with that role. If you play a charismatic person, you inevitably discover aspects of your own inner light in order to express that character.

I have heard from some people who have never acted onstage who think that performers do it for the applause they receive, but actually that is the most boring bit. I always found the applause awkward, because for the curtain call you have to walk onstage as yourself. It was much easier for me to be someone else in a different story. There is no editing when you play the role of another person. You don't have to worry about how that character is being perceived in everyday life. It's all permissible because it's part of the script. I loved how acting could liberate me from the conflicts in my own life.

Acting also gave me a sense of my personal value because I was giving value to others through a skill I had. I loved that. By the time I got to drama school at nineteen years old, I had already done fifty stage productions. So when I graduated at the top of my class and then quit acting a year later, it was a big shock for my family.

"I'm not doing it anymore," I declared.

Understandably, they just couldn't wrap their heads around it. But what was happening was that I was starting to get more outlet for expression in my life. I was beginning to discover who I was and no longer leaning on the crutch of theater. It was a slow process, but I was discovering that I was okay. I could be who I was in the world.

Theater wasn't my only area of interest in my teens. My curiosity about metaphysics and spirituality was becoming greater all the time. One of the tools I gravitated toward was tarot cards. From the first time I encountered the tarot, I remember just loving it. I would go to receive a reading and my whole body would feel alive. I think some people approach tarot or other kinds of intuitive readings simply as reassurance in the face of an uncomfortable now. I can understand that. If you're not comfortable in your life and you hear a few good things about your future, you relax, and there is a power in that for people. But for me, it was actually *more* than just that. There was something mysterious about the whole process that I loved, and I wouldn't find out until later what that "something" was.

When I was around nineteen, I was gifted a tarot deck by a good friend. I never learned how to formally read the cards, but I would occasionally play with friends in an improvisational way. I would throw some cards down and see what came to me. By the time I was twenty-two, I had done this on a handful of occasions, and the weird thing was that each time, my friends would remark on the accuracy and power of the information they received. So although I didn't think my readings were "real" at the time, they were really helping people.

This was a sign of things soon to come. This was the beginning of destiny calling.

❧ ❧ ❧

One month before the Zs began communicating with and through me, another mystical opening took place. I had just moved to London for work, and my dear friend and soul sister Nina came to visit. Nina and I shared a keen interest in all things metaphysical and esoteric, so I was intrigued when she told me that she had recently begun dowsing.

"Dowsing — what is that? I've never heard of it," I confessed.

"Let me show you," Nina said excitedly as she reached for her bag. She took out a small quartz crystal on a chain.

Standing in front of me, Nina held the chain between her thumb and forefinger with the crystal dangling motionless at the bottom.

"First, you hold the pendulum like this," she said. "And then you ask a question. The crystal will start spinning to give you your answer. If it spins clockwise, the answer is *yes*, and if it spins counterclockwise, the answer is *no*."

Nina demonstrated with a question of her own, and the pendulum started to spin, quickly giving her an answer. I totally thought she was faking it. She was holding her hand perfectly still, but the pendulum was spinning at high speed. I wondered how the hell she was performing this magic trick in front of my eyes, as it couldn't possibly be real. I trust Nina with my life, but as she stood in front of me with a crystal spinning on a chain, my inner skeptic showed up in all his glory.

But then Nina handed the pendulum to me.

Secretly rolling my eyes, I held the chain still and asked my question. In a matter of seconds — lo and behold — the pendulum did begin to spin all by itself. First slowly. And then wildly. I was blown away.

Within one week, I was using it every day and had become a believer. Soon I came to know in my body if the answer was a yes or no before the crystal even started spinning. I also began receiving more than just yes-or-no answers. Using the pendulum as an access point, I started to receive intuitive messages when I would ask my questions. I can look back now and see how this pendulum practice was opening my intuitive mind.

Around that same time, I bought a book called *How to Connect with Your Spiritual Guide*. I can't remember who the author was and haven't been able to find a copy since, but that was the title — and, truth be told, I never actually read it. I was noticing how specific book titles in your living space or surroundings can work as affirmations of intent. For example, if you have money issues in your life and you buy (but don't read) a book called *How to Love Money*, just having that in your environment exerts a power all its own. It can have an energetic effect on your life. Under that principle, I enjoyed the presence of the spirit-guide book near me but never really thought I would get in touch with *mine*. I wasn't at all sure that I even had any spirit guides.

Then came that morning on the London Underground.

Without realizing it, I was gradually opening up a field of communication with the invisible world, and a phenomenon that I had never imagined possible for me was picking up momentum.

On that fateful day, after the Zs had interrupted my negative self-talk by telling me that I was wrong about what I thought was happening in my relationship, the conversation continued.

"Is this my own head?" I asked.

"No. We are your guides, and we are indeed talking to you."

"I've never heard you before. Why now?"

"We've been talking to you for a long time, but you weren't ready to hear our words. And today you are."

"Am I schizophrenic? Are these just voices in my head?"

"You're welcome to think that, but no, that isn't what's going on. If you work with us for a few months, and if you ask us questions and see how our answers fit with you, you will see that there is help we can offer you."

By the time the train reached my station and came to a stop, so had the conversation — and I didn't feel alarmed by it at all. People often ask, "Was it *weird*?" And the weirdest thing is that from the very beginning it *wasn't* weird. Don't get me wrong. It does feel different. But it makes sense to me now that when the channeler and their guide or guides have aligned, it shouldn't feel strange. Some people imagine that channeling is an out-of-body experience, but for many channelers I know, including myself, it's a uniquely *embodied* experience. If I channel for an audience, for example, or if the Zs come through me to speak to someone in a private session, then yes, it does have a bigger impact on my body than when I do it for myself. My body grows hotter, and I can sometimes get more tired if I go for a long time.

I took the Zs up on their offer and began writing down questions for them to answer. It was a fascinating few months. One thing that really struck me was that the guides never stroked my ego in their messages. They would give me helpful and supportive information, but they would also tell me if I was off base about something.

For instance, they would say, "No, this isn't your partner's problem. This is your problem. And we'll explain why. You are struggling with your need to be right. And if you let go of your need to be right, you will see the wisdom in what your partner is saying to you."

I would write that on the page and walk away, and the next day I would revisit it and reabsorb it. It would change me.

For months, I did this for myself alone. But eventually, I shared this process with a few friends who were spiritually inclined, doing sessions for them with the Zs and sometimes speaking intuitively rather than channeling. Initially, it was something I kept very private. I didn't tell my family — only my more open friends knew about it — because it was something I was aware could be perceived as weird or freaky, and I wanted to avoid being viewed that way. When you have been the fat kid, and then the person who has to come out to his friends and family as gay, you don't necessarily want to come out as the channeler, too.

But bigger for me than my own personal fears was the truth of how the Zs were touching people's lives.

They were helpful.

They were loving.

And for me, they felt like home.

In 2000, soon after I began channeling, I took a memorable trip to Glastonbury for the big music festival that takes place there every year. The company I worked for was fund-raising for Greenpeace, among other charities, and Greenpeace took forty of us to the festival. It was an amazing group — social and environmental activists, artists, and other progressive people doing really interesting things. We would fund-raise for a part of each day, then enjoy the music and festivities the rest of the time.

That weekend I offered to give my friend Niall a palm reading, of sorts. I don't quite know what possessed me. Like the cards of tarot, the lines on the hand were something I knew nothing about.

I just took hold of his hand, held it in mine for a few moments, and then gave him the information that intuitively came to me.

"How did you know all that?" he asked incredulously. "How did you know that about my family and my past?"

It was a powerful experience. And word that I could do this spread fast around the company. I was slowly beginning to grasp that beyond my ability to channel the Zs, my own capacity for reading the energy of a person, situation, or place was increasing.

I had been channeling for about a year when I started to go to personal development and healing seminars with some regularity. One that I remember vividly was Psychology of Vision, led by Chuck and Lency Spezzano.

There were about 250 people in the seminar room on this particular day, and Chuck posed the following questions: "What if God knew best how to use you, and you let go of your own agenda? What if you simply said, 'God, use me,' and trusted that whatever happened to you next would be right for your life?"

Then he said to us, "Step forward if you're ready to do that."

I remember that a lot of people in the room didn't like this suggestion. Several didn't step forward, evidently reluctant to surrender their own agenda. On the other hand, many rushed forward, clearly all about surrendering and trusting the path. Then there were those of us somewhere in the middle. I liked the idea of stepping forward, but I also had other ideas in mind for my life.

I thought I was going into music.

One of the reasons I'd left acting is that I had discovered songwriting at the age of twenty-one, and it was "love at first song." I had just released my first self-funded album and was hoping to get it picked up by a record label. So I was more than a little hesitant to say, "God, use me," in case he didn't use me the way I *wanted* to be used! I wanted to travel around the world playing music that would open people up, because music for me had been such a lifesaver. Ever since I'd been a kid, it was the one place I could *really* feel things. To me, sad music was not sad. It was life giving, because it took the sadness I might be feeling and animated it, moved it through my body, and gave it room to breathe. I wanted to do that same service for others through the music I was writing.

The irony, however, is that on that day I *did* say, "Okay, God, use me."

And I stepped forward.

This was six months before I started doing intuitive readings for people in addition to the channeling. But it wasn't until many years later that I realized the full scope of what shifted that day when I took that step. I had given myself permission to deviate from my desired path of music, yes. But I have spent the past thirteen years going around the world helping people open themselves up, holding workshops where those openings can happen within a container of safety. I've created countless audio recordings where my voice helps people open to who they are. So although my focus is not being a singer-songwriter, the effects of my work are exactly the same as those I hoped to achieve musically. I still love music and make music, but my aspirations for it as a career are being fulfilled completely through my spiritual and self-growth work.

I got to the desire underneath what I was trying to manifest as a musician. And I basically got that career, just in a different form. It's funny how life works, isn't it? Our prayers and intentions get answered — just not always in the form we think they need to take. It's therefore no small surprise that when I am teaching people to manifest their dreams, I always suggest that they understand the desire behind the form. For example, you want to manifest money because you desire more freedom in your life. Sometimes it's more powerful to write an intention that affirms "I wish to manifest financial freedom" than it is to write "I wish to manifest a million dollars" — as you never know what unexpected pathways financial freedom may take to arrive at your door.

❧ ❧ ❧

When I started doing readings in June 2004, I certainly had no idea I was at the beginning of a brand-new career that would not only bring me great satisfaction but also pay my bills.

The moment that kicked the door wide open came after I did a reading for Anaiya Sophia, a yoga teacher, shaman, and good friend. Over coffee, I helped her and her then partner with a challenge they were wrestling with, and soon after that she came back and said, "Wow, that information really transformed things for us. Thank you so much. You should do this as a job." I have to admit that I thought she was just being kind.

But she persisted.

"Lee, I have a newsletter with three hundred people on it. If you write an advertisement for your sessions, I will send it out to them." I genuinely didn't believe that anyone would respond, which was partly why I said yes. I had no idea that the day Anaiya's newsletter went out, I would get my first paying client.

My session work started small, but word got around quickly. By the end of the first sixty days, I had done readings for sixty clients from around the world. They would send me three questions by email that would take me seventy-five to ninety minutes to answer in writing. And after a year of written readings, I went to telephone and Skype.

From the very first reading, I was so moved that someone I didn't know would trust me with their private, innermost thoughts, feelings, desires, and fears. It was a deeply intimate process. In those early days, whenever I received someone's questions, I would move really fast to write their answers, because I felt a huge sense of emotional responsibility to them. It would often make me cry to read their questions. It opened my heart to be trusted in that way, to be confided in, to be invited into their inner worlds.

I didn't tell my family I was doing readings for about eighteen months, until it became too hard to hide because it was about to become my full-time vocation. As it turned out, I had nothing to worry about. My brother's wife, Anna, received one of those early tarot readings before I ever did this as a job and has been a part of my administrative staff since 2011. My brother has been greatly supportive all along and has lent his marketing and business skills to me many times over the years. And my parents and the rest of my family are always very sweetly proud of me whenever they attend my events in London. I'm truly grateful for their support, especially as the realm of spirituality and self-growth was not necessarily their world.

If my work has taught me anything, it's that no matter where people come from or how much money or success they have, everybody is human; we all have the same fears, hopes, concerns, and dreams. Each of us has something in life that we are challenged by — regardless of how things look on the outside. That was such an eye-opener for me in the early days of my work. Several years in now, I have had many clients who have reached the heights of outer-world success, in terms of wealth, fame, and accomplishments. As I have walked with them through some of their hardest moments, I've seen firsthand that no one — no heart — is immune to the adversities of life. We all get hurt. We all suffer at times.

There is much talk about how we as human beings are pre-disposed to suffering. And in the spiritual community I often see people trying to undo their own suffering, while simultaneously hoping (and praying) that once it goes, it will be gone forever. One of my passions is to support people to have greater awareness of their issues and points of pain, and to find new ways to be *alongside* them. To end the war with their suffering and befriend it instead. To "soften" around its presence. To allow positive change and healing love to occupy more and more space inside, while the "issues" lose their power.

The benefits people receive from my live and recorded work are the same ones available through the pages of this book. They include:

- Emotional self-awareness
- Clarity and discernment
- Forward momentum (a.k.a. getting unstuck)
- Empowerment (powerful self-permission)
- Self-trust and confidence
- Optimism and enthusiasm
- Opening up intuition and empathy
- Connecting deeply with spirit
- Comfort and joy
- Transformation

Our energy fields are far bigger than our conscious minds. And there is a whole range of color and feeling around each of us that intuitive people (and people who are opening their intuition) can pick up on. That, to me, is where the magic of the universe really arises and appears. So much around and within us is beyond what we can see with our eyes.

The infinite is everywhere. Literally.

Energy speaks all the time. We just need to learn how to listen.

I have never believed that personal and spiritual growth takes place on a mountaintop, in some kind of holy isolation. It usually occurs in the ordinary moments of our lives — and often through the support or mirroring of another person. I believe that we all help each other as human beings. If a taxi driver smiles at me on a day when I'm not feeling very happy, that person can change my mood. The energy of that smile, that love, offers me a potential upliftment. That's a simple example of how someone we don't know can help us.

When a healer or practitioner works with us in an in-depth way, holding our hand through some of our most challenging or difficult moments, there is yet another kind of "helping each other" going on. The willingness to trust someone to do that, and their ability to compassionately be there for us through our process, is such a beautiful way to heal and to grow. Of course, we can grow every day we live, but personal development work is a deep and powerful accelerator of our growth.

I have always highly valued personal development in my own life. I spent my twenties going to workshops on credit cards — whatever it took to get me there. I remember wondering, *Why are some of the happiest days of my life spent standing in a room with hundreds of people who are crying one minute and laughing the next?*

Now I understand. I felt really *alive* in those environments back then. And that remains true today.

But unbeknownst to me, I was also training for the work I was going to do.

Now I'm a custodian of those very types of workshop environments. I did a world tour in 2016, traveling to Australia and then on to events in London, Berlin, Hawaii, and twenty-eight cities across North America. I met over five thousand people at these events. Many lovely people along the way told me they had copies of the first two self-published volumes of *Energy Speaks* by their bedside. They talked of how they would just flip the books open to a page, looking for guidance, reassurance, or a fresh insight. Hearing this touched my heart and reminded me of the power of the energetic frequency of the Zs.

This was significant because at the beginning of 2016, I was questioning whether it was time to stop publicly channeling, whether or not that phase of my work would now be available simply in archives. During the tour, I got confirmation that the channeled portion of the various events added a frequency all its own to the work we were doing. When I channel, it changes the energy of the room in a very particular way. For some people, channeling is an important part of the work that I do. All together, the intuitive work, music and sound healing, physical movement, and channeling produce a lovely balance of multidimensional energies for people to find themselves in and through.

It was the tour experience that prompted the desire to take those first two books and make them into something brand-new — the very book you are holding in your hands right now. This is the ultimate edition of *Energy Speaks*, including new material derived from both channeled sessions with the Zs and live events where the focus was my work as an energy intuitive.

Of the many lessons I've learned through working with the Zs all this time, perhaps the main one would be the power of intention — that you can cast an intention for what you would like to experience and feel next in your life. They have taught me to trust that writing that intention down on a piece of paper, affirming it verbally, and calling it to mind repeatedly will help bring it to you at the time you are ready to receive it.

Each page of this book — whether focused on relationships, abundance and manifestation, angels and spirit guides, or any other important life topic — is really a reminder that we *do* cocreate with the universe. We can either be asleep in that cocreation or be *active* in it. There is a destiny path at work *for* us, and we have free will as to when and how we step onto it.

May *Energy Speaks* support you and inspire you as you embrace the destiny path that was made only for you. You have absolutely no idea where life can take you or how things can change for the better, so never stop dreaming.

And when destiny calls, perhaps in an unexpected way, I implore you to *listen*.

CHAPTER 1

YOU ARE A LIGHTWORKER

Owning Your Personal Power

This chapter is adapted from my first-ever channel to a public group and is still one of my most enjoyed and frequently recommended channeled recordings. Our group gathered in June 2006 at a beautiful small retreat property in France, near Rennes-le-Château. There were yoga classes led by Anaiya Sophia, and I would work individually with participants, in addition to leading group ceremonies in some of the incredible sacred places in the area.

I will always remember the feeling I had after delivering this message: I felt altered — very different in my body, somehow energetically rearranged. What was then a novel experience (being a messenger for a group) would soon become a familiar and far more natural-seeming occurrence in my life.

Welcome, powerful people. You are all powerful, mightily so. And today you seek to be reminded of your own power, power that is your inherent right. You came here as powerful souls with messages to share with the world. You are lightworkers. We do not say this to everyone, but you are. It is the work of awakening in consciousness that you are doing — that you deliberately came here to do.

This planet needs as many of you as possible to create the consciousness shift now occurring. And how you feel it! It can feel beautiful, wonderful, joyous, humorous, light, fun. It can also feel torturous and wretched. The shift involves a whole spectrum of emotional states. And in order for consciousness to evolve, this full spectrum must be experienced. You are experiencing the spectrum at various levels of awareness, but the whole shebang, as it were, must be gone through consciously so that the shift can be completed.

This is what you all want.

Your work as lightworkers will challenge you. Oh yes, very much so. Lightworkers need to be at the top of the wave and surfing it, scouting ahead so that everyone behind can swim in clear waters. When we say "behind," we would suggest that you not get caught up in status. A lightworker is no better — or less — than a human being who is *not* actively working with the light. It is just how it is. You are no less or more important than the next person. You are a unity of souls. And every soul has their crucial role to play. So be mindful when you judge, for in judging you temporarily separate yourself from your expanded human family.

Competition between lightworkers is being cleared and eliminated at this time; it is one of the final arenas where battles need to cease for this evolutionary shift to occur. As lightworkers, you will sometimes compare yourselves to others. Good. Do it. Experience how it feels, but do it consciously and with awareness so that you may become free of it.

Judging yourself for such comparison and competition will not free you. Being *aware* of this dynamic as it arises in you will help to do so, for you can then experience the emotions intuitively, intelligently, and honestly — as a way to quicken your growth. You will be able to facilitate the movement of these dark feelings from within yourself. They are part of you. They are part of the world. They are not to be feared. They are simply to be allowed passage through you, for you do not need to harbor them anymore.

You need not see yourself as moving up the levels any faster than your fellow lightworkers, racing against them. You are simply at various stages of focus, discovery, and the implementation of your gifts. Imagine if everyone were at the same place — standing on the same rung of the ladder. Progress would be impeded. How would humanity as a group be able to move forward?

WHAT DO YOU BELIEVE ABOUT YOUR POWER?

Recognizing and owning your personal power is one of the most important steps you will ever take as a lightworker — and a defining moment in your development.

Personal power is not easy for human souls to embrace, for it is not easily embraced in the world. Many of you wrestle with the profound responsibility that standing in your own power demands. It is contained in nature, however. Parts of the world that have been heavily abused by man still hold power. Where a rain forest has been destroyed, there is still great regenerative power in the land. That power cannot be denied. It cannot be permanently stripped.

Whether denied or admitted, it is the same with the human soul. A soul has great power and arrives in human form charged with that power. The experience of life can convince the soul to minimize this power or to give it away. And this perceived lack or loss of power can lead a soul to try to regain it through the domination or abuse of others and the attempt to take power from others. Of course, we say "attempt" because you can take nothing from another soul. Just as *you* cannot really give yourself or your power away, either.

It is all a matter of beliefs.

And as you know, beliefs are powerful. Beliefs can imprison or free you. Beliefs, along with the thoughts and ideas derived from them, can convince you of anything. Where your personal power is concerned, you have choices to make on a daily basis — about accepting it, allowing it, expressing it, and directing it — and you will continue to have to make those choices on an ongoing basis. What do you believe about your power? What must you believe about your power in order to operate at your full capacity?

As your consciousness rises, pay close attention to your beliefs, for they are a crucial key to your expansion.

A CONSCIOUSNESS SHIFT

You have within you a jigsaw puzzle. It is all there. All the pieces are there — beliefs, attitudes, thoughts, feelings, experiences, desires, dreams, purpose, destiny, and more. Your outer life offers manifestations of this inner jigsaw puzzle, allowing you to see the picture that is keen to emerge at this time in your life. As it does, you can put the pieces together — and move them around as you wish — so that your jigsaw puzzle becomes whole once more. So many jigsaw puzzles — so many lives — have been incomplete for too long. This incomplete picture can feel like a drain of your power and energy.

The reason why some of you are finding this time so hard is precisely because you are shifting — growing and transforming in profound ways. And in the flux of change, the jigsaw pieces can sometimes seem scattered to the wind. Yes, much has been said and written about a period of great change that was imminent, but the difference is that this awaited shift is happening now.

Right now.

This period of time has long been designated for a shift in consciousness affecting the earth for many years to come. We speak to you now of personal power because that is what is required to navigate this challenging period. Do not feel that you are a victim of the energetic change occurring. Oh no. Remember, you chose this. We say this to you with caring and affection, for we understand how difficult it can be as a human being when you experience pain, heartbreak, uncertainty, or the fear that arises when stepping into the unknown. It can be challenging to maintain your understanding of the larger truth of what is going on, both in your own life and in the world at large. But do choose to remember. Remembering brings you back to the seat of your power and brings greater ease to your life experience.

YOUR INTUITIVE POWER

You are very powerful intuitively, but you are also afraid of the strength of your intuitive power. It is not surprising. Your intuition is an agent of change. Allowing the subtle and overt truths told by your intuition into your life more consistently will cause energetic shifts in your body. It will cause you to feel different and to see the world differently — but that is wonderful. It will make you more whole. It will make you stronger. Do not fear your intuitive power, for it is already so. You are only asking us to say this to you as a reminder, because you know it yourself...and you feel it.

Exercise: Connecting with Your Soul Power

Here is a brief exercise that can energetically prepare you for your day and positively charge you up for every day to follow:

Allow yourself to feel the energy that exists right now in this moment in your body.

Ask your soul to give you a taste of how much power and energy this body can house for you. Allow your body to be shown a glimpse of how much is within you and how much could be within you if you let it in.

Then allow your soul to return you to a state that will benefit you most in this moment.

ALLOWING JUDGMENT AND FEAR TO FALL AWAY

Remember, time is so important. It is your ally. This is why we speak to you of releasing judgment. Do not judge yourself for not being where your soul knows you should be. It is important to move step-by-step, to integrate every piece of your journey. What satisfaction would you feel in going from being a disassembled jigsaw puzzle to a completed one in the blink of an eye? Who does that? Those who do that do not find a great deal of satisfaction. The joy of a jigsaw puzzle is the piecing together so you create the whole picture. It is a fascinating game, full of stops and starts, sometimes maddeningly complex and sometimes a breeze. There is satisfaction when the whole picture is complete, yes, but the piecing together — *that* is the discovery process of life. That is where the energy lies.

You all have so much to give. Your hearts give out so much love to the world. This is true even of those who doubt it. You have no idea how much love you share each day. Some of you judge yourselves for not giving enough, and some of you judge yourselves for giving too much, as you question your motivation for giving. Some of you judge yourselves for not being able to know if you are giving or not, because you're not sure of the impact your giving is having. Trust us. You are all giving so much.

Now receiving — here is an even trickier area. This is the area that many of you would deny. Layers of conditioning cloud your relationship with receiving. *Who am I to receive more? What have I done to deserve it?* However, receiving is where more giving becomes possible. Really. You all deserve so much.

We feel *you* now, and you are the most beautiful, wonderful, giving soul. If we could only somehow allow you to see that for a moment, we would be so happy. You are divine.

Now is the time for you to remember. Remember. Remember. Remember. Aren't we boring? We could say "remember" to you constantly because it is all we want you to do: to remember how much light you are already giving out to the world. Stop working at it. Instead, work at developing your connection to all that is. Work at doing whatever makes you feel closer to the God within you — this source of power and love within all of you. Do whatever you feel inclined to do. Far be it from us to tell you what to do. We would never do that. We hope you would never take anything we say as prescription. We only ask you to *remember* that you are already doing the work.

So much judgment comes in for you — you fear that you are not fulfilling your purpose, you think you are not completing your mission, you worry that you are not there yet. Tell the mind to quiet down so the soul can relax. The soul may very well know where you are going, and you can tell the soul if you need a little while so that you can reach that place in your own time. You will be no good to anyone if you jump there too fast. You will certainly be no good to yourself; you would be thrown off-balance. You are a lightworker, yes, but you do not need that disruption. You do not need to become exhausted and weary on your sacred journey.

SOUL GROUPS

Trust that where you are now is so perfect. And keep reminding yourself of that daily. Reach out to fellow lightworkers. This is not the time to stay alone. You are all surrounded by your soul groups, and they will expand and grow in the years to come. You will bring in more and more soul friends: lightworkers, yes. But right here and now, you are surrounded by the groups you need to help you develop. Receive them. Make a choice to allow these people to become visible to you, and do not judge yourself if you cannot yet see them in your life.

If you are greatly struggling with this, then do this brief exercise with us for a moment. We will go in a little deeper and see if we can help create some energetic movement for you....

Exercise: Identifying Your Soul Group

Place your attention and focus on your heart chakra — the energy center of your heart. Do this gently and in your own time, and if at any point this feels uncomfortable to you, stop and try again at another time. Do not force yourself to do anything.

Allow your heart chakra to expand. Allow yourself to feel it growing wider, bigger, and stronger energetically. For some, this will be very apparent, very strong. For others, this will be subtler. There is no right or wrong. Just allow yourself to feel the expansion.

Once you feel the expansion, ask yourself to be shown the faces of those people around you who are your soul group, your lightworker compadres. Some of these faces may shock you; some may not be who you were expecting. Some of them will be miles away from you, in another city, state, province, or country. It is all fine. They do not need to be living with you or showing up at your house for dinner every evening. See who they are and understand that you are connected to the people you are seeing. If you are having difficulty seeing anyone, we suggest you try this exercise another time. Keep trying it, because the faces *will* appear.

As you see the faces of this group, ask your heart to tell you what each group member brings to you in your life. What are the gifts that each person offers you?

Some of these faces may be challenging to you. Some of them may be your worst nightmares. Breathe...and allow yourself to see how they, too, have been great gifts to you on your journey. Identifying them as gifts will allow you to step out of any emotional or psychic holdings you have with them that are now unnecessary. This is not the time for battling lightworkers. Although you may still have some battle left in you, this is not the time.

Hear that.

And if hearing that brings up a great urge to battle, commit to going through your battles to release them. Battles in this context are energy fights. They are where the energy shifts from one person's ego to another's. So you throw your energy at the ego of another in response to them doing the same to you. It gets you nowhere, really.

Standing in your power: that is the antidote. So if one person tries to throw their ego at yours, you simply stand in your truth and provide an energetic barrier to that occurrence. You do not even need to push them back. You can stand in the depth of your knowing and a robust boundary will automatically rise to protect both of you.

You might be asking us, "How does this experience manifest in real life? I hear your words, but I do not fully understand. It seems too abstract." Consider this: how do you feel when someone suddenly enters your space without your permission? This could be a subtle entry or not so subtle. There could be a slightly uncomfortable feeling in you, almost too faint to detect. Or it might be that the person punches you in the face, which may be the kindest way, actually, because it's an undeniable breach. The other way is harder to discern.

Establish the boundaries that you need, but stop fighting. That is what we ask you to do, and not because we wish to give you a rule but for your own sake.

And if a mighty war breaks out between you and another after you have agreed to this, then that is no different from what is happening on your planet, is it? You are not solely responsible for planetary wars occurring simply because you are involved in a personal fight. But you are contributing to that conflict energy. We are not making a judgment on war; we are observing what is happening. It is important to see what you are shaping as an individual, as a group, as a world. Become curious as to what is playing out in your outer world on a global level. Be wary of judging anyone in the outer world.

Use our words for your benefit, but do not judge yourself against them. That is not what we ask you to do. You are beautiful, but so is everyone in the world. There is not a "bad" person in the world. How terrifying a thought is that? Yes. Because suddenly that changes everything.

LOVE IS THE LIGHTWORKER'S WAY

We have given a little food for thought, and the final thing we wish to say to you is this....

If you do only one thing in response to our words, thank yourself. Thank yourself for choosing to keep on shining your love. It is not an easy choice for you to make in the current climate of your world and given the trials and tragedies that you may have endured. It has taken terrible heartbreaking experiences, great personal sacrifice, or a feeling of often being isolated and alone. But you have kept leading with your heart.

Thank yourself for doing that.

And look back along your path and see how you have managed to do it all this time, against all odds you have faced in your life. Recognize that you are still here, and more than that, recognize how you are shining a light for other people.

The experience you are having as a human on the earth is set to change. And one very powerful way to recognize how well you have done is to acknowledge that it will be far easier from now on. You have survived the most difficult period you will have gone through.

We take a risk in saying this, don't we? But it is true.

The consciousness of your planet is raised, and you are a

lightworker who has played an instrumental role at this monumental time.

You will not always be joyous every moment of every day, but you will never again view the pit as quite so dark, or feel quite so helpless, for you have identified who you are…and you have found your heart. That is a great gift both for you and for the world. Be patient with your heart. Be patient with yourself, especially on emotionally cloudy or stormy days. They, too, can be beautiful days.

The heartbreak of this planet is healing. It may not seem so, but it is. So, lead with your heart, both for yourself and for others. Where you share your love with others, you are leading with your heart. And where you lead with your heart, you are demonstrating to others how to open their hearts.

Remember your connection to your source power. You have this connection now. Use it. Simply turn toward your heart and ask for help if you are feeling lonely or struggling. Open your heart and ask for love to enter it, and it will. It truly will.

With that, we wish you our love. And we wish you *your* love, for your love is even stronger than ours.

And we invite you to connect with the hearts of every other person reading this. Allow yourself to open your heart to more of your energy family. If you wish, place your attention on your heart chakra, in the middle of your chest, and in your mind say, *I connect my heart with every other reader, every other lightworker reading these pages.* Open to that widening connection and allow yourself to feel the power in that. Feel the strength and solidarity in that. Feel how full you are. This closeness and connection are yours anytime. You can come back to this divine feeling as often as you would like. This divinity is yours.

In peace and with love to all.

Closing Exercise with Lee: Calling Back Your Power

As the Zs have said, it is time to call back your power. You cannot ever give your power away completely, but you can leave pieces of you outside yourself. You can ask others to carry those pieces of you — the friend you believe is stronger than you are, the colleague you believe is more disciplined, the lover you believe is more capable. But these are your pieces. This strength, this discipline, this capacity for living — it all belongs to you. You recognize in others pieces of yourself, and it is time to embrace and integrate them. It is time to own them. It will not take away from the people you see these qualities in, not at all. Your ownership of them will double the strength of these qualities in you and them.

Sit or lie down and be comfortable where you are. Take a slow, deep breath, and let yourself relax.

In your mind's eye, see a vision of another version of yourself sitting directly ahead of you, a few feet away. You are surrounded by white light in a clear, almost translucent space. This "you" has their back to you and is sitting very calmly, very happily.

Now, on behalf of this "you," say this statement aloud to the universe:

I call back every piece of myself that I have ever given away.
I call back every part of myself that I have identified with only in others.
I own all these pieces.
I bring back all these fragments.
They are mine once more.
They are in me. They connect me to the universe.
This is my power.

This is my surrender to my power.
I call back all my power.

In your mind's eye, see this "you" and all these pieces you have called back reintegrating into your body. See the body ahead of you, this other you, being filled from every direction, every corner. See the color and light flooding into you.

As you watch this process unfold, *feel* it. Feel yourself being filled. Feel whole and full yet light and expansive all at the same time. This is you. This is yours. All this is who you are. All that you now feel is who you can be all the time. This is your power, and this power is yours to carry.

This power is yours to rest within.

This power is you.

The Lightworker Affirmation

My work is clear, no matter what job title I hold.
I awaken consciousness in the world.
I awaken compassion in the world.
I awaken love in the world.
And my work always begins with me:
As I recognize and honor the divine source within me,
those around me are inspired to do the same.
This is my gift as a lightworker.

CHAPTER 2

YOUR SELF-LOVE JOURNEY

"*Your Self-Love Journey*" *is adapted from the transcript of a weekend workshop in 2010 in Berlin where the Zs took a practical approach to self-love. Because they recognize that self-love is often experienced as an elusive future goal rather than a present-day reality, they offer a "challenge" — a simple three-week plan for prioritizing self-love in action. This channel is a favorite of mine, in large part because it's based on the understanding that self-love is a choice. As the Zs say, "Choosing self-love is the ultimate act of mastery because it has the power to bring all aspects of your life into alignment."*

I hope you enjoy the opening relaxation exercise for quieting the noise of the mind in preparation for receiving yourself at a deeper level.

Opening Relaxation Exercise

Take a deep breath in and out, connecting with yourself and finding a comfortable position as you drop further into your body.

Listen to the sound of your breath as it flows into and out of your body. Let your breath be soft, compassionate, and accepting of everything happening in and around you in this moment.

Feel this self-breath filling your belly, expanding your chest, and connecting you with all that is.

With your next breath, allow yourself to become the most important person in the world, at least for now.

Just breathe...and feel the safe space that is evolving in-side, making room for more of you.

Put your hand on your belly and feel the connection you have with this sacred place in the center of yourself. Feel the warmth radiating from your hand and into the soft, vul-nerable, and powerful center of yourself.

Breath by breath, feel the self that is so deserving of your love.

You are ready now to begin the self-love journey.

SELF-LOVE IN ACTION

Self-love is the subject of many books, poems, songs, workshops, and to-do lists. "Get more self-love." Check.

On the one hand, it gets diminished, like a quaint New Age idea for people who have the luxury to think about such things. On the other hand, its importance can get elevated to a point where it becomes almost mythical — "the impossible dream." Our intention is to help give you access to more self-love now and over time, practically and consistently.

It is true that there is a lot at stake when it comes to loving yourself — you sense that. You feel the call to self-love largely because it unleashes your full potential. Your *full* potential. And that is a very big deal. The world needs your full potential because you are a lover, a healer, a change maker, and a lightworker.

One of the myths about self-love is that it can happen in an instant — or overnight. For most human beings, it is a long-term affair.

It's a relationship with yourself.

So the day you commit to self-love, you might feel great at first. Then there comes a point, maybe two or three months down the line, when it will start to go a little deeper for you, and old patterns and beliefs can reinsert themselves. It's just like a new love affair with a person: "We were great for three months, and then we lost it — he wasn't available anymore," or "I just didn't feel it anymore."

It's the same with self-love.

As with a relationship with another person, the big "secret" to success is to keep committing to being present and to be self-loving even when things aren't going well.

You are not a stranger to self-love, we know. However magical or lonely or difficult your childhood might have been, you wake each day and you parent yourself, even if you don't recognize that you are doing so. That is one way you love yourself. You dress yourself in what you like to wear or, in some instances, in what you like the world to see you wearing. You eat the foods that are pleasurable and, in most cases, nutritionally valuable to you. And just like your actual parents, you probably don't parent yourself perfectly. That's okay. You can make incremental improvements starting right now.

Your journey of self-love is so informed by the love you have experienced with others — parents, siblings, lovers, teachers, mentors, coworkers, and of course, friends. No matter what your age, it's possible you still feel that you have never been loved by another in the way you have always wished to be. This can be the case whether you are currently married, used to be married, or have been single more often than not.

If you feel that you have never been seen, heard, held, celebrated, and loved the way you want to be, it is time to turn your attention inward. It is time to marry yourself for a little while and see what changes that will bring in your external relationships as well.

As you read this chapter and make use of the exercises, you will discover that a great act of self-love is to find out what is *purely you*. What thoughts, feelings, perceptions, expressions, creations, needs, desires, and dreams are purely you?

To help you find these answers, we lay down a challenge to you: to devote three hours a week for three weeks to your self-love and self-care. This is three separate hours across each seven-day period where you do something you love or discover something new that you didn't know you would love. Ideally, you will step beyond your usual routines and experience something new.

If you already have a good practice of self-love going, reevaluate it after you have read this chapter and see how you can change or increase your self-loving activities.

THE 3-WEEK SELF-LOVE CHALLENGE

Welcome to the challenge that will take self-love out of the realm of philosophy and fantasy and make it very real.

First, open up your calendar and decide what your start date will be. When would you like to begin to feel more love?

Next, we recommend reading this chapter in its entirety before scheduling your specific self-love practices and activities. While you can do anything your heart desires during your three hours each week, we have some insights to share with you on the topics of *time and space*, *nature*, *touch*, and *creativity*. The information that follows will help you design and shape the challenge in the ways that will nourish and uplift you the most.

During your chosen self-love time slots, turn off your cell phone and computer. This must be about you and your senses without external communication, for the most part. Of course, if you're getting a massage or having a counseling session, you'll communicate with your therapist. But the primary focus is you loving *you*.

It may be far harder than you think. The internal demand to "get it right" or do it perfectly could arise, but the important thing is your willingness to try it. This process will give you new insights into the way you work, the way you see things, the way you feel things.

Our hope is that it will be the exhalation moment you have dreamed of for months, or maybe years. This simple structure will help you prioritize yourself and will provide the relief that you keep thinking you'll get one day soon — maybe next weekend, or when you go on vacation, or when you retire.

The wait is over.

Before you even complete the three-week challenge, you will be resetting your vibrational frequency and reaping the rewards of doing so. You will be much less likely to get knocked off-center by energies that aren't yours. When you're walking down the street, driving on your highways, or watching the news on TV, you won't lose connection with yourself. You will find yourself laughing more, dreaming again, and feeling the magic of life in and around you.

You will find out that focusing on self-love is an act of great generosity. The more filled up *you* are, the more you will have to give and share with others.

Time

If you are feeling tired, uninspired, or down, you can make powerful shifts in your energy during the challenge by putting attention on *time*. In fact, we have devoted *extra* time to the topic of time because changing your relationship with it can be completely transformative.

When it comes to time for yourself, most often the response is: *There isn't any time!*

"I have a lot of responsibilities — at home, at work, in my life. I never get time for myself."

Where time is concerned, we would change that word *get* to *take*: "I never take time for myself." This immediately moves you from being a victim of circumstances to being the empowered creator you are.

It is imperative that you take time for yourself if your current experience is one of lack in any area of your life — if you feel that something is missing. Turning your focus onto yourself for the coming three weeks will begin to change the perception that anything is lacking.

Time and Space

At the beginning of the three-week challenge, make a list of everything that you are truly not enjoying doing but can easily let go of. Commit to letting go of those things.

If you are not enjoying doing something that is more complicated to release, allow yourself to simply hold an intention for that thing to shift. Sometimes, if you are longing to release a relationship or situation where there are several reasons why you cannot, you may feel quite frustrated. This angst can cause you to forget that you have options and possibilities. You forget your magic. You forget that you can say (either out loud or silently), "I wish to release this," even if you don't yet know how that will happen. Surrender the "how" to the universe in you, and it will create a way, at the speed you are ready for.

If you are saying, "This is all well and good, but I have a busy life, and it's not going to slow down in the next month or two," know that that is a lie of the mind, albeit a very convincing one. You can find three hours in one week that you can time-table. If it works better for you, you can parcel those hours out into thirty minutes a day over six days.

If you can't do this, you are in a state of energy slavery to others.

If you experience frequent burnout — where you expend all your energy for as long as you can and then, suddenly, you need to take a day off and collapse — that is a lack of self-sustenance and self-maintenance. You can change this during your self-love challenge, one choice at a time, one day at a time.

Taking time for yourself is the same as making space for yourself. And making space for yourself opens up your receiving energy. In fact, making space for yourself may be the missing piece you've been looking for as you attempt to put the puzzle together for having a balanced, abundant, and more joyful life. If you are willing to create and keep more space in your life, you'll receive more options, opportunities, and choices. And then you get to select the ones that feel good to you.

Pay attention to the phone calls, emails, and text messages that suddenly come your way when you start taking time and space for yourself. Notice *who* is calling, writing, and texting. Are they the people in your life who often want your attention or drain your energy — each giving you an opportunity to practice sticking to your boundaries? Are there any commonalities and themes in these communications? Are you seeing old patterns and programs mixed with new energies and dynamics?

What are you saying yes to? What are you choosing?

Follow your feeling.

If you need to be tempted back into taking less space for a few days, trust that. But we do recommend that you slow things down and run everything the mind is telling you through the wise filter of feeling. This is challenging if you're not used to it. But see how your feeling self informs you.

Life on Earth is busy. Start to take more breaks now in order to create a different template for your future relationship with time.

Here is the big secret....

No one will notice or mind.

At first, that will scare you. You'll realize that some of the things you thought were so important to you and others were not so important after all. They were simply happening because you decided to let them happen.

Your world will rearrange itself around your choices. And you have nothing to lose, because you can always go back to the old patterns if you don't like the new ones.

Time and Work

Work. This is a very powerful word, for it is an area in which many people find themselves comfortably stationed, even though things can get uncomfortable. Within your work — as a parent, entrepreneur, CEO, caregiver, teacher, or manager...or whatever your position or role may be — you can find yourself overgiving on a regular basis. And this overgiving requires a great deal of your time.

You could be someone who genuinely enjoys giving your energy to work and to other people. You are here, in part, to create with your energy through your work and the way you give to others. So, where giving time to yourself is concerned, we have good news. You need only make a small adjustment to receive huge benefits — like the three hours per week recommended during this challenge.

Self-love time does not have to mean you are completely alone during those segments. However you spend this time, one of the most important principles is that you begin to understand that you are in control of your calendar. It may not feel like you are at times — when deadlines, responsibilities, and loved ones are calling for your attention — but the choices are yours.

One of the first things you'll see transform will be your abundance. When you're vibrating at a place of surrender and trust, your needs get met. However, if you're on the hamster wheel of believing that a certain amount of money or a certain type of home will give you the time and space you're craving, you are probably very tired right now.

In your commitment to love yourself and prioritize yourself during the three-week challenge, you will gradually stop feeling weighed down and overused. Your practice of giving yourself three hours a week (even if you need to work up to that) will change your relationship with time, space, yourself, and others. And you might overhear yourself using words like *more, plenty,* and *enough!*

Nature

If you feel that you need more space in your life, one of the fastest and most effective ways to find it is to put yourself in nature. A mountain trail, the bank of a river, a sandy beach, a wide-open field, a canoe on a serene lake — even a patch of grass — can be a self-love remedy. If you live in an urban area, as a sensitive individual you will feel better by visiting a small park in the city center. If you feel good there, it will refill you.

You're living in a fast-moving technological world, and yes, while the energy body can transmute almost anything when it is working up to its full potential, you are still processing electromagnetic and other frequencies the human body has never had to deal with before in the past. There is nothing in the memory code of the human body, passed down from your ancestors, that has had to deal with such frequencies on Earth.

Love yourself back to vibrational harmony, especially if you work a great deal with computer energy.

With nature, you can restore balance. With fresh air, you can restore balance. Nothing beats fresh air for clearing your energy field and physical body, even if it's the fresh air of a city like Beijing. This is very important to remember. It is not a luxury to go for a walk in the park; it is a necessity. It is no less important than eating or sleeping. As you embrace this truth, your experience of life will get easier.

Balancing your own energy system has to become a focus when you are at the level you are at — a conscious being who is here to grow and to be a force of love on this planet.

Let us be clear. We're not saying that nature will take away all intensity and suffering. But it will greatly support you and allow your mind to be calm. Your mind gets very busy when your emotions are activated. Take the mind for a walk at these moments. Take the body for a walk at these moments.

Where do you like to go walking that is easily accessible to you? Think of somewhere you can get to fairly easily on most days. Currently, this is one of your power zones, a place where you feel your power. It may not be one of your power zones next month or two years from now, but you will know when it no longer works for you. For now, go there and recharge.

The physical body needs grounding at this stage of your awakening. You will always feel that something is missing if you're not grounded, so in this way, grounding is one of the keys to self-love.

If at any point you are going through a release, you don't even have to think about what you should do or where you can go for relief. You have programmed it. *I told myself I'd go to the forest when I need to walk through something.*

You are putting yourself in motion and taking action. There are two different types of action, depending on how you feel: If you are experiencing a lot of energy, you might find a vigorous walk really beneficial. If you are feeling strong emotions or are lost in thought, take a gentle walk. The important thing is to move the body — move your energy.

You might be resistant to doing that, but if you can just give it a go and try that a few times, you will start to change the pattern and welcome the energy release.

Touch

Your body needs touch, either your own or another person's. Self-love is not only an emotional, mental, and energetic need. It is physical as well.

If you have been alone or without partnership for an extended period of time, you could be experiencing *touch hunger*. To put it simply and directly, this is when your body is hungry for love — love that feels like connection, care, attention, sweetness, tenderness, affection, warmth, passion, or compassion. To feel the touch of another's hand on your body or the warmth of an enveloping hug can transmit these feelings, and more.

Many people who have been single for a long time get into a downward spiral of thought. They wonder what is wrong with them that they are not attracting a mate. Sometimes, they have simply gotten stuck in this place of touch hunger, and reawakening those energy senses opens the floodgates of connection.

Whether you are single, happily partnered, or somewhere in between, you will benefit in countless ways by making touch an important part of your life. After the three-week challenge, you will likely choose to keep making it a priority.

Start with self-touch. If you've never done it before, try caressing your body. Try literally hugging, cuddling, and holding yourself. Gently stroke your hair, your face, your arms, your legs, your feet, and — especially — your belly. Your stomach area is deeply receptive to your self-loving care.

If you can, schedule a session with a skilled massage therapist or bodyworker of some kind. Allow yourself to be supported and "held" by another, without any type of agenda other than your body receiving healing, caring touch.

And do not be surprised if, while on that massage table, a wide range of emotions, thoughts, and memories move through you. The energetic movement will help reconfigure you and bring greater ease to your body.

Creativity

When you hear the word *creativity*, what comes to mind? Many people think of art, especially the fine arts, such as painting and sculpting. But whether you are gardening, cooking, writing a letter, teaching your child the ways of the world, leading a meeting at work, or having a conversation, you can bring creativity into it. You can make the way you do anything an art form.

Creativity is simply using the body to bring something through, to create something with your energy.

Neglecting creativity can bring sadness, because the life force within you is designed for expression. There is a great urge to communicate, reveal, and share the unique spark of consciousness that you are. Creativity is a way to give — oftentimes to both yourself and others.

In what ways are you most creative?

In what ways or in what areas of your life would you like to be more creative?

Creating love itself is one of your greatest abilities as a human being. Generating more and more of this essential vibration is a profound art form. As a creator of love, you can multiply and amplify that energy and infuse it into everything else you create.

Creating from this love inside you is one of the reasons you are here.

You *love* love, and you miss it when you feel it's not there, when you're not feeling it in other people or you can't quite feel its presence in yourself. Create something that holds the vibration you wish to experience. This does two things: (1) it brings an immediate soothing to the soul (you're not waiting for an outside source to fulfill your wish), and (2) it widens your energy field of love. This sends a message to the universe as to how much love there is in and around you, a flow of energy that will not run dry.

There will be times when it will feel good to give your love to somebody who is in need, a family member or a friend who you can see is in a desperate place. You and your abundance of love will happily and effortlessly bathe them in comfort.

Because creativity is a way to say "Yes!" to all the powerful life within you, it is a great act of self-love. And, in truth, there is no shortage of this force within you. As your self-love challenge will affirm, the more energy you put *into* loving yourself, the greater your energy *output*.

More creative expression — during one of your three hours

each week, for example — is another way to give yourself positive, transformational energies. Draw, sing, dance, write, daydream, brainstorm, paint, doodle, bake, stitch, glue — express yourself in any way you feel inspired to.

All the powerful, loving energies you stir within you when you consciously focus on your creative expression have a mighty effect on your body, mind, and emotions.

Initially, you may find that your moods shift very quickly. Anger, rage, happiness, enthusiasm, serenity, melancholy — any of these feelings, and more, may mix and mingle within you like a kaleidoscope of emotion. As you acclimate to new energy pathways, especially as you send your own creative energy back into yourself, the furnace that resides at the base of your body will rev up. It will produce more creative fire and amplify the energy and love in you.

Let's do another open-eye visualization to stoke your inner flame, starting now.

Energy Meditation: The 5-Minute Flame

Visualize the sacred furnace inside you. It sits between your hips, at the base of you. You can feel the energy coming from this furnace that is quite present and alive. Arising from this furnace is a flame, your own inner fire.

Let the tip of this flame start to rise, until it reaches your belly button. The tip of the flame comes to a fine point. If you follow the flame down, it gets wider. While its tip now reaches your belly button, your flame is spreading below, filling your abdomen.

Keep letting the flame rise until the tip reaches the center of your chest, your heart chakra.

Now that the tip has reached the heart, see how your belly and solar plexus are being filled by the flame.

As you feel the nourishing and expanding warmth of your inner flame, you also sense things being consumed by the fire — limiting thoughts, beliefs, feelings, and patterns that don't need to be processed with the mind.

Just breathe into the belly and allow this burning to take place. Let the flame fill the hollow of your stomach with positive, powerful energy.

As the widening flame engulfs the center of your heart, feel that flood of tingling energy as your heart wounds are mended.

Now, let the flame continue its rising. The tip is traveling up from your heart toward your throat, simultaneously filling your shoulders with its healing heat.

Breathe into it.

Feel how full your body is now, suffused with pure life-force energy. With aliveness. With passion. With creative energy.

Breathe that in. Feel the warmth. Feel the joy. Feel the love.

Now, allow this loving flame to permeate your skin — clearing and cleansing as it reaches gently beyond your body, connecting the inner and outer layers of you.

Feel the warmth of your inner flame touch your cheeks and warm your whole face. It's not uncomfortable; it is enlivening as it reactivates your cells.

Now, let the flame rise up and over the top of your head so that you are enveloped in this constantly moving soul flame from your hips upward. Let the energy grow all around you.

When it is fully surrounding you, feel yourself encased in this "egg" of fire. This is your power. This is the flame of life within you — the fuel for your creative self-expression and your ability to share your love.

For another minute or so, allow yourself to be bathed in this flame. Absorb this fire. And feel your energy pathways opening.

Sense the perfect union with the self.

And now, send the flame downward, back through your throat, heart, and stomach, and then down to your knees and through your legs, traveling to your feet.

Let the flame get smaller and smaller now, until it coils once again at your base, between your hips. Take your time; there is no rush.

Finally, place one or both hands on your stomach to help integrate your experience.

Slowly breathe in and out, thanking your body for taking the self-love journey with you in this lifetime.

Attending to your energy field is the same as showering or dressing each day. You may get very cross with yourself when you feel you're back in an old pattern. If you're experiencing any upset of this kind, do a little energy work for five to ten minutes each day — morning, night…anytime you feel that you're off-center. It will reset your energy field very quickly.

Wrapping Up Your 3-Week Challenge

Tending to your time, your connection with nature, your need for touch, and your innate urge to express yourself and create, you will find that your world will look and feel very different by the conclusion of the three weeks. However you choose to focus your time and attention, these are practical doings — increasing self-love through action.

With each minute and hour, you are building small worlds of love, wherever you feel the need for them.

Each time you keep your commitment to yourself, you are making a choice to build your energy. So, create physical spaces for yourself (in your home, at your office, in nature) that are recharge spaces for you. Use creativity to flow love through your body. No matter how chaotic your environment or the world may look, be a guardian of your love and give yourself peace, a little every day — for when you are a guardian of your love and peace, you will attract other guardians to you. When your energy is low, when you are in need of support from another person, such as a loving conversation, you will carefully select whom you go to.

As you open and surrender more to self-love, you are in the ultimate union of your own male and female energies. You're also evolving these energies. In this way, your self-love journey will positively affect and upgrade every relationship in your life. From the inside out, you are becoming a guardian of love itself.

RELEASING HEARTBREAK AND GRIEF

As you take this journey into deeper self-love, you naturally start to release old heartbreaks, and grief can come up in the process.

From childhood, adolescence, and adulthood, old wounds of not feeling loved can surface. Know that they are revealing themselves so that they can move through you.

As you change your vibrational frequency through self-love practices, the types of mates, friends, and cocreators you will now attract will hold the new frequency. And the deeper into self-love you go, you will find yourself naturally letting go of that which no longer serves your growth and well-being.

The idea of losing more than you already have can bring up fear, for you have been through loss and know very well how it feels. But the truth is that loss awakens gratitude within you. And letting go makes room for new beginnings and deeper love.

It can be confusing when one day you are consumed with grief and you do not know why. You will experience these releases in two different ways: you may be powered up in one moment... and feel weighted, heavy, and tired in another moment. Recognize that this is the process, and remember that others have gone through the process, too. Amid the highs and lows, you will be okay. You will move through it all.

When grief arises, remember to breathe. Breathe *through* the grief. *Move* the grief. Take it for a walk, take it to nature, take it running or into stronger activity if you feel you have lots of adrenaline and energy surging through you.

To be self-loving is to let go of suffering.

Some days, you might need to dive into the feelings in order to get through them. But also tune in to your innermost wisdom when you sense that you might be in a pattern that's keeping you in a loop of suffering. This is when it can be best to ask for support from another person — a therapist, bodyworker, life coach, spiritual counselor, or other helping professional. Seeking the service and help of others can leave you strong, empowered, and energetically clear.

COMMUNITY: INTO NEW WORLDS OF LOVE

As you get filled up from within, we recommend that you get out into the world and experience this feeling more proactively. If you have some fear of this — because your energy sensitivity has been high — you will be surprised by how quickly you'll realize that your vibration has changed, especially if you have been spending a great deal of time alone. It may shock you to see how easy it is to be out there, amid your human family. More importantly, it may surprise you to feel the marked expansion of the love you feel for other people.

Enjoy the new feelings. Open your arms wider.

Community is beckoning — those you already know and new energy communities. Keep your eyes, ears, and heart open to connect and receive.

It is an old cliché, quite a well-worn expression, because it is so true: loving yourself will attract great love to you from others. And you are increasingly capable of engaging with more love, coming from many directions. As a boundary, just be aware of the hunger for love that exists in many people. Sometimes this hunger may make them want more from you than you can give. Their wounds may see you and your energy as their source of freedom and healing. You will know when it is right for you to say yes and to say no. Continuing with self-love practices will help you be centered in yourself and able to be close to others in healthy and uplifting ways.

Being a part of close, conscious, and creatively alive communities is one of the gifts of the self-love journey.

Sacred Commitment Ceremony

In closing, we invite you to a sacred ceremony, a commitment ceremony with yourself. This is truly a divine partnership, a marriage of the masculine and feminine aspects of yourself. A marriage of the light and dark within you. A marriage of the fearful and courageous parts of you. A union that celebrates your wholeness.

In your mind's eye, see yourself standing at an altar in your best wedding outfit. And whether you choose to have a solo ceremony or one surrounded by all your loved ones, notice that the hands you are holding are your own.

Take a slow, deep breath, feeling the irreplaceable wonder and miracle that is you. And now, say the following vows to yourself, allowing the universe to hear your intentions, dreams, and promises:

I promise to love myself.
I promise to continue to learn more about loving myself.
And when I am not being self-loving,
I invite my soul to show me this.
I promise to give myself the freedom to explore this world,
to do everything I want to do.

I choose to experience myself at higher levels.
I choose to turn my focus away from pain and struggle.
I choose effortless living,
turning my focus toward joy and peace.

I will give myself space to discover who I am.
I love myself so much that I allow myself to make huge mistakes.
I love myself so much that I will always forgive myself.
I trust in my love for myself so much that I know that

whatever situations I end up in, when I remember to feel
my way through them —
rather than think my way through them —
I will always come back to the place
I need and want to be in.
I vow to honor, love, and cherish my body and my soul,
always.
And so it is.

Self-Love Energy Exercise and Affirmations

Write the following sentences in your journal, and make note of the thoughts and feelings that follow.

I am the most incredible person I know.
If I die tomorrow, I know I have achieved
the extraordinary in my life.
Thousands of people have been positively touched
by me and my love.

Breathe.... Each of these sentences is designed to move energy in you. If you feel resistance to any of them, just notice that feeling and the beliefs attached to it. See what is on the other side of the resistance.

CHAPTER 3

THE ART OF RECEIVING

This was my first full seminar in Germany, taking place in December 2009, and I chose to focus on the topic of "receiving" — not simply as a basic human capacity but as an art form that can be developed and refined over time. In my work at that time, it was frequently pointed out that the area of receiving is a place we human beings don't trust and that giving is generally far easier for us to do. I appreciate that for some people the opposite may be true, but as a general pattern, this is an issue I see a great deal in my work, and I have seen it in my own life. So this channel was a joy to ask for, and then to deliver.

Welcome to a conversation on the art of receiving. It takes a while longer to energetically prepare Lee for such a talk — and so it is with most humans. This topic brings up the internal knots and limitations, and it challenges your perceptions of living, giving, and loving. Indeed, receiving is intertwined with all areas of life, affecting work, finances, living situations, and every relationship you have.

This is an especially appropriate month in your planet's calendar to look at the art of receiving, for today is December 5. Twenty days from now, people will be unwrapping their presents, receiving their gifts. Yet it is interesting that this one day of receiving can create one to two months of organized chaos before it, including actual fighting in stores! People can become quite aggressive when they go Christmas shopping. It is not just because the stores are busier; it is because there is an energy of fear and pressure around all this giving and receiving. With an enormous amount of giving during the holidays, so few on Earth at this time have the balance of receiving.

How often have you found Christmas to be a mighty disappointment (purely because of the expectations that have been placed upon it)? You may well have given up on the tradition of Christmas that you used to hold dear. The tradition that would see you putting endless energy into cards and presents — exhausting yourself on top of your already overfull workload to amass this giving to others, only to find that it was all over within a few hours.

There can be beauty in giving a material gift, for it is an offering from one soul to another of something that may hold value for them. That is wonderful. Understand that what we are pointing out here is how the pendulum needs to swing the other way for people to truly enjoy Christmas or other occasions to give that are meaningful.

THE GUILT WOUND

Ask yourself this year, whatever time of year it is when you are reading this, which way is the giving-receiving pendulum in your heart swinging? Are you allowing yourself to receive as much as you give? Are you feeling guilty because you needed to cut back on some of your giving compared with previous years?

Guilt.

An interesting word.

It is one of the great wounds where receiving is concerned. Guilt can stand in the way of feeling deserving of receiving, and it is often what drives people to overgive when truly they do not wish to give at all or are too depleted to give — for example, the mother who feels guilty for being tired after spending one hour with her child. Really, she could do with some rest or twenty minutes to herself. But she will use guilt to mobilize herself into thirty minutes of play with her child because of how bad she feels that she was not so present the previous hour or was a little angry in her words. And during this thirty minutes, she is not authentically there; she is just exhaustedly trying to repay her supposed sin. But there was no sin. She was just tired. She couldn't give any more. And the child understands this energetically.

Let's do a brief exercise to release guilt and open the doors wider to your receiving.

Exercise: Releasing Guilt

How do you feel right now when you think of the word *guilt*? Can you feel it in your body? Can you locate it? If you can, that is wonderful. It means you will move through the guilt very quickly. If you don't feel it anywhere in your body, that is also wonderful.

If you can feel a knot of guilt, you may sense it as akin to a large rock in your stomach. Or it may feel like a small knot in your heart or just to the side of it. See and sense this as the illusion that it is. Place your hand over the part of your body where this supposed knot locates itself.

If you are feeling the knot outside your physical body, in your energy body, allow yourself to place your focus upon it. Whether the knot is body-based or within your auric field, send energy to it from your heart, feeling the light you have there, which is like your inner sun. Allow that sun to grow and radiate until it burns through and melts this knot away.

Do not worry if it feels difficult or the knot seems stubborn; just do what you can. Allow the light to permeate it. Allow your hand to gently help move it away. You needn't carry knots of guilt, yet they will be there at times. Even if you are already quite good at saying no and maintaining your boundaries, you have likely been receiving mastery tests recently. Happily, these tests will now create only tiny knots of guilt, where before there would have been a great chasm of guilt.

Allow guilt to be burned away, no matter what the source. You are so very deserving of freedom from the energy trap known as guilt.

As we move on from this topic, please stay with any knots that you feel need more work.

Do you trust everything that might come to you? Or are you living in fear that what you might receive could put you through your paces? If you have been going through an almighty release for a long time, you may understandably be a little shell-shocked, a little traumatized — feeling that it is not safe to open the doors to the unknown or the unpredictable.

Have a conversation with your mind and see if it is in a state of recoil. Is your mind in fear of receiving anything new at this time because of how overloaded your system feels?

It is important to look at potential blocks in this area, because there are many gifts coming your way — even as you read this. What is occurring today is that you are being given some help to open to receiving a little faster than perhaps you would otherwise. You're getting a boost of understanding about how you operate energetically.

THE LIMITLESS LANDSCAPE OF YOUR LIFE

Having options is a form of abundance. Consider for a moment the options that you have right now. Do you have many, or do you feel bereft — as if you are a member of the No Options Club at this time? If you feel angry that there are no options — like you are up against a wall and have had *enough*! — trust us when we say that this is the place many of you reach before the options materialize. When you arrive at anger after a long period of exhaustion, stress, or trauma, that is often the green light for *go*. If you feel frustrated, you are about to birth yourself into a new reality of options. So, if you do not see your options yet, just visualize a few anyway. You know what it is that you would like to experience even if you do not know exactly what it should look like.

Exercise: Opening to Options and Possibilities

What are your current money options? If you are frustrated because of a lack of money, imagine some in your mind's eye. Make it as large a sum as your body can take without combusting, of course. Do take this number high; it will help with the exercise.

Then bring up another option, something that will fulfill you on a relationship or career level. And then another, something that will bring more happiness to your daily life; it might be having more time for taking walks or for friends. Anything you wish to add, bring it in. This is an exercise in opening your feelings to allowing *more*.

In your mind's eye, your inner vision, see these options in front of you and consider them one by one. Turn your attention to any one of them to begin with. How does it make your body feel? Do not be convinced that what you experience within the first minute or two will be your experience three or four minutes later, because you may have to burn away some feelings to get to the essence.

For example, if you have been offered work that you are unsure about, it is quite likely that when you first place your attention on this option, you will be burning away your lack of certainty. It is a little like rolling the dice — you don't know what number you will end up on, but it is definitely worth burning away that uncertainty to find out. (Remember, this is a private exercise to see how you truly feel and how much you can open to receive your divine inheritance. The exercise will not commit you to anything, but it will stir possibilities within you.)

There is a strong connection between stomach and heart. So notice how your stomach feels. And then notice how you feel at heart. The heart is generally where your joy and your passion lie. But if there are trust wounds, the stomach will be churning with anxiety, fear, or a sense of unsteadiness before the heart can open to the option. Place your hand on your stomach if this is happening to you.

If you are psychic and are receiving information about this future possibility, you may have a slight burning sensation in the third eye — the energy center above the brow, between your two physical eyes. So again, if there is any discomfort anywhere, place your palm facedown over this part of your body. It will help. *Good.*

As much as possible, keep your focus on this one option for a while. And when you have finished with it, move to a second option — and even a third.

There is nothing in life you would wish to experience that you do not deserve. If you want something that you currently don't have, it is never about deserving. Where the word *deserving* appears, guilt is usually around the corner or behind the scenes — the idea that people can be guilty enough that they do not deserve.

Guilt can be moved along and released, for guilt is only an energy of discomfort held around past actions. And the past is the past. The past is gone. The child whom the mother feels guilty about has already moved on to another focus of attention minutes later. (Of course, this is not true for every child. Often, the older a child becomes, it is true that they can hold on for longer periods of time. But this mother metaphor is key for all of you, because you are quite extraordinary in your capacity for feeling the responses of others yet sometimes using this sensitivity against yourself by feeling guilty.)

There is often a "lack" mentality on Earth, as if one person receiving what they want will deny someone else what *they* might want. You see this in larger families or families where there is a shared belief that only one person can have their turn at a time. That can sometimes be appropriate for a family that is challenged financially, or challenged around other important resources, and is trying to make sure all is fair for everyone. But if that was your situation in the past, you have moved on from that family system now.

Now you are free to receive everything.

You are free to receive as much as you want.

You are free to receive yourself.

HONORING YOUR CHOICES

As you start to access that freedom, it can be an extraordinary experience, even euphoric at moments. But it can also be a little ungrounded at times because it is new. New levels of freedom have to find a place in the body to inhabit in order for the feeling and principles to become fully operational in a human being.

Fear about opening up into this euphoric state can surface. Euphoria is a very powerful energy to adjust to. And sometimes there is fear about receiving everything that comes your way. Everything can feel daunting, especially if previously during a time of great openness you received five things and two or three of them left a sour taste in your mouth or turned out to be not so good.

That is why it is so important to choose with the body in the present moment and to allow your body to feel good about everything you choose. If it does not feel good about something you are choosing or if it doesn't yet know which choices to make, then do not choose until your body is ready.

If there is a pressure to choose something that you have not yet said yes or no to, you will be notified of that pressure, either by your body or by the party offering the choice. Sometimes the greatest gift you can give yourself is to take your mind off it and distract yourself, especially if you are going around and around in circles.

As for those options that do feel good, is there any hesitation about stepping toward them? Is there hesitation about receiving that much good? Or do they remind you of something that backfired in the past? The little voice in your head usually goes something like this: *The last time "this" choice felt good, "that" happened a week* [or three months] *later.* The body remembers. But the body also clears itself quickly. The mind is the commander of the body until you stop it from being so. And like all good generals, the mind takes its guardianship of the body very seriously. The mind will do everything it can to protect the body from future hurt based on past experience.

So, the more open you become to receiving, the more crucial it becomes to demote the mind from its leadership position. You are now taking bigger and bigger leaps each time you give yourself something or allow yourself to receive. And in taking these leaps, you can have three, ten, thirty, or a hundred thoughts that the mind has to let go of — little notes to self made the last time you got burned. Here is where the mastery test comes in: Do you listen to and become consumed by the mind? Or do you recognize that when the mind is running on a loop, that is no longer who you are? Yes, you can experience mind loops sometimes — the lessons they offer are part of the awakening and ascension process for so many. But *you* are not a mind loop. And you do not have to remain stuck inside a mind loop.

You are in your body, in your energy, and you are full of feeling — more than ever before.

Pay rapt attention. That feeling capacity can lead you to your most beautiful life.

FEELING: THE GOLDEN KEY TO RECEIVING

Know that sometimes when you are in a mind loop, this is where your attention has been asked to go temporarily to resolve one of those knots of guilt. If you are one who empathizes with others acutely, these knots of guilt can arise when you feel their pain — especially if you tell them no or do not give them what they want. You feel a pain, a sadness, or a sense of loss in them. This is because you are not going to be the person they have just pinned their dreams on, and at a certain level of awareness, you both know it. There is some measure of pain for the child you had to say no to, or for the person who just asked for your hand in marriage who is about to be told no.

It is not easy to witness other people's pain and feel that you are the cause. This is what happens to sensitive people. Sensitive, empathic people have a hard time saying no because of what they feel in the other person when they do. Often, this is when little knots entangle your energy field. If you feel other people emotionally or sense them energetically, you are "wide" in energy. You would not be able to do so otherwise. The width of your energy field across the table when you said no to the marriage proposal enabled you to feel the implosion in the other person. And as you walked away, you took a little bit of that energetic memory with you, if it served you to do so.

It is beautiful. There is no mistake. You are doing it to clear yourself of the feelings of others, as well as heal your own unresolved feelings. And so many of these relationships are what you would call karmic; they are contractual. What gets left inside the body from these karmic relationships is often hidden but can be released. When you do an exercise to clear yourself, allow yourself to feel whatever is there. And if you cannot feel anything, just imagine. Let the mind show you. The mind will pull up a story for you. It will show you the trust wound.

The story is all about love, always.

OPENING TO LOVE

Love is the highest level of feeling that the human body can experience. There are many different ways to experience love. Receiving is a heart-opening, love-expanding act. When somebody gives you something — be it a material possession, their attention, a smile, or some other expression of their energy — and it touches you, your heart opens a little more.

If you have been going through difficult times and people give you love, it can bring forth tears in you very easily. Their love is helping heal your woundedness, your contraction, in that moment. When you are wounded as a human, you contract and draw everything in. All your energy goes toward dealing with the part of you that was left with a hole.

If a relationship ends, leaving an almighty hole, you may spend months recovering so that you can open your heart once more. If you can open to receive it, love will come to you from others as you go through the grieving process.

Do not be hard on yourself if you have spent six months grieving. At the beginning, it may be that you can receive loving support only once a week. Your body may be temporarily shut down to that flow. But as you go through the weeks, you will open to receiving more and more.

TRUSTING YOUR BODY

Think again of the person you might say no to and how that might affect them. Think of what you feel in that moment, and understand that your sensitivity can make you nervous about receiving. In opening to another opportunity or to another person's giving of their love, you are not always sure what might follow. For example, within a romantic partnership, a moment may come when you unintentionally get triggered by the other person.

This catalyzing act will cause your greatest wound to be replayed, whether that wound is rejection, anger, attack, or confrontation.

But here is the point: you have already done an enormous amount of — that word you love — *work* on yourself. (Of course, every moment you are alive you are working, which is why there is some humor in that word to us. Working is being. Doing is being. It is just a different way of focusing your being.) Having done this work on expanding yourself, you are so much clearer now. It is often the mind that holds the fears. If you can start to identify this and trust that it is the truth, it will make your choices in the coming times much easier.

If one week from now you are offered something and you go into fear, notice where the fear is located. Is the fear in the body or the mind? For example, you are invited to your friend's party and, without much thought, you say yes. But as soon as the "yes" escapes your mouth, your body starts to decline the invitation. You do not feel good about going. It just does not feel right. You don't know why, and that feels strange. If this is what the body is doing, trust the body. And even if you arrive at the front door of the party, you can choose not to go in if you still feel the same way.

The mind is somewhat different. If you are invited to the party, your mind may go into hyperdrive, saying things like *The last time I went to a party there, nobody spoke to me, and I got stuck in the corner with that annoying woman who wasn't listening to a word I said while she kept telling me about her misery. She wasn't even feeling her misery, but by the time I left the conversation, I was feeling it.* A barrage of thoughts like these is the mind's undoing.

Start to notice the difference. Whether it is your mind "undoing" or your body giving you a true reading, there is no judgment. But it is time to know the difference so that you are not caught in a vicious circle. You do not need to be. You are an energy master. You can understand energy. What you gain and enhance when you own your energy mastery is your trusting relationship with yourself.

Trust this body of yours. You have spent all this time clearing it, healing it, emotionally freeing it. Now trust it. Your body did not let you down in the past; it was trying to show you that you are sensitive, trying to help you pick up on the signals in and around you. All that is different for you now compared with the past is that your mind did not previously pay conscious attention to feeling and to energy in the way it does now. It followed the map laid down by previous generations — which, until the 1990s on your planet, was fairly limited in its scope of feeling. In that decade, the feeling and the energy sense started to open up. You see it everywhere, referred to by many different names. Some call it spirituality or awakening; others call it a collective conversation on emotional healing and integration.

RECEIVING YOUR DIVINE INHERITANCE

The reason we are so joyous about delivering the art-of-receiving messages in this channel is that so much of your work has already been done. We are simply rallying the troops — already trained and more than ready, just exhausted and crying a little, not quite realizing that everything is right over the wall.

It is joyous for us to deliver this message to you because all we are doing is showing you what you have already achieved — and that is lovely. It is a great gift to be able to reflect to a person how extraordinary they have become. And while you are all at slightly different places, you are within the same zone of actualization.

You are all here to receive a great deal. And nobody else out there can tell you what is right for you. They can give a perspective. We can give a perspective. But your own body is the one to rely on. Learn to trust the body. Learn to trust the feeling in the body as you continue to clear so many of the old emotions and wounds. You are then truly free to receive. And understand this: the more you open up, the more options you will receive — and more regularly than you used to.

ᘏᔭ   ᘏᔭ   ᘏᔭ

In closing, place your hand on your heart, and say inside yourself, *I am open to receiving my inheritance. I am open to receiving my love.*

Your love is always reflected back to you in the love sent through and from others.

And now say, *And so it is done.*

For indeed it is.

The universe is a little like a bank with branch locations all over the place, and you are constantly investing your love here, there, and everywhere. It multiplies your love and offers it back to you all the time through other routes — other faces, other events, other experiences. If you are focused on receiving only in certain areas and from certain people, especially those who are often the recipients of your giving, you might miss the person knocking on your front door. You might refuse them at first because you have given this stranger nothing, and you do not even recognize who they are. Yet no one has a problem with Santa, oddly enough, even though no one has ever met *him.*

As a child, you quite loved this idea of a man who had never met you who came around and gave you a bunch of presents. He did this every year, for free, for you. Children have no problem receiving in that way.

Santa is the universe. Father Christmas is the universe. And the universe wants to give to you. But you do not have to take every single thing that is offered — you get to choose what you are here to receive.

In peace, and with love to all you receivers.

The Receiving Affirmation

It is safe to open my heart to receiving.
It is safe to open my arms to receiving.
With ease, I am receiving my soul's inheritance.
With joy, I am receiving love from every direction.

CHAPTER 4

ABUNDANCE

"*Abundance*" *was the second-ever channeled recording I made with the Zs, recorded in January 2006. I was doing mainly private readings at the time, so creating a recording was a new frontier. But what I remember was the effect that it had on people who heard it. And that gave me confidence to continue.*

Back then, there was a growing focus in the transformational community on how to manifest what you want. The movie titled The Secret *was just about to launch, and the hot topics at the time were money and abundance.*

In listening back to this recording, I recall feeling that my guides took a slightly more holistic approach than the one found in some of the material on manifesting and abundance I had been exposed to. To me, the concepts delivered here felt much bigger than simply manifesting a car or another material possession. I remember feeling that this channel offered a way to reach forward and create in the future, while also reminding us to feel grateful for our abundance in the now.

We have the power to shift our reality and create differ-
ent lives for ourselves — if we choose to believe and envision
it. That is at the heart of the Zs' message, which I would call
directional living.

Abundance. This word carries so many connotations within your society. There are many misleading beliefs and ideas — so many *un*-abundant experiences — associated with this word.

What does this word mean to you? When you think of the word *abundance*, what is the first thought you have around it? What is the first image? The first feeling that you connect to it?

For some, it will be spiritual wealth, meaning living in an enlightened way with connection to spirit, with connection to source and others, as a daily experience. For others, it will be wealth on the material plane — money, personal belongings, status within their work or career, and the acquisition of material objects. There is a great difference between the two.

A truly abundant life is one where there is surrender. That is the key — true surrender to everything. Surrender to allowing a great wealth of experience, of financial resources, of love. And also a true surrender to experiencing the opposite of this state — for example, lack. If lack is the truth you are experiencing in any given moment, then lack is what you have created for yourself for the growth of your own soul.

The way to achieve true abundance is to surrender to the place you are in now, while always investigating how true it is that you are holding yourself in that place. This is just as important for those who have material wealth as it is for those who do not. For, more often than you might imagine, those who have material wealth are maintaining such wealth at great cost to themselves and their happiness. It is a wealth they are maintaining based on the fear of no longer having money, losing their career, or losing their position within society. And this lack of surrender to life, this need to control, creates an un-abundant inner reality.

The truth is, the universe will deliver to you your abundance. Another truth is that many will not receive that abundance from the universe because of their belief system, because they have limits in their minds as to how much they can receive, how much they are allowed, or how much they deserve.

ABUNDANCE AND KARMA

So let's look a little deeper. Abundance and karma are very tricky bedfellows, as it were. You see, karma can directly affect your abundance in each and every life you live. So if it were to be your karmic desire to experience a life of lack on the material level, that will be the reality. However, as with any karma, this process can be sped up if you learn the lesson.

If your karmic lesson is to let go of the need for material wealth or status, then once you have achieved this and truly let go, your karma is done. The lesson is over. It has been rebalanced. You can move on, free. Karma and abundance go hand in hand in this way.

The opposite can also be true: there are those humans who have decreed they will experience a great deal of material wealth, man-made wealth. They, too, experience this until they have learned the lesson, and then it can all change. So, you see, everything is possible. Everything is open to change. However, certain lessons must be learned before these possibilities become available.

Bear this in mind if you appear to be in an experience of one extreme or the other where abundance is concerned. In either situation, the best you can do is surrender. Surrender to the experience you are in, all the while remembering you are fully entitled to experience the opposite. The full spectrum of having and not having is available to you.

FREEDOM FROM THE WIN-LOSE PARADIGM

Abundant living is when you are fully on your path and truly receiving all that your life wishes to offer to you. This could manifest as a great partnership, great material wealth, great spiritual connection, great work that fulfills and nurtures you as much as it gives to those around you, great love of nature, or simply a great life experience upon this earth.

All these states of abundance are achievable at the same time, but in your current society the energies of competition and comparison are dominant. Therefore, many believe that one of these states must be forsaken in order to experience the other. For example, one commonly held belief is that you are entitled to either a great partnership *or* great wealth, but not both at the same time. Certain countries and cultures have a higher regard for this rule of competition than others, imposing strong limiting beliefs upon the state of abundance for individuals within their societies. You need only look at your own country to know where it falls along the spectrum. It will not be hard to work out.

But the greater truth is that all is possible. Every single soul living on Earth could be experiencing far more abundance were they not trapped in agreement with this man-made world, this world where money has all the power. And, of course, for those who have money, for those who are in the business of making money, the *need* for money gets stronger. For the more they achieve it and the more it does not fulfill them, the more they want it — and the deeper their need for it. In this way, many are unknowingly attempting to replace spirituality and spiritual fulfillment with money. Money becomes a drug that they can never get enough of, because money alone cannot replace connection with spirit — the real need.

Those who do not care about money — those who see money as a by-product of their lives, who have a healthy disinterest in it — they are the abundant ones. And this works one of two ways. Either they do not mind that they survive on little in comparison with other members of society, or they are achieving ample money for themselves while not enduring the stress and tension of being overly focused on money.

So, to understand abundance and increase your possibilities for creating it, you must first strip down this world you live in. This human world is currently not simply one of free-flowing abundance. It is one of possibilities *and* limits. There is a hierarchy in operation, one that has been created by mankind and decrees that some people win and some people lose. And while you are in service to and in agreement with this hierarchy, your experience will be exactly in alignment with it: some will win and some will lose.

Once you have collectively healed and expanded beyond this — have understood at the level of soul that this way is not the truth — then a new way for the whole world to move forward together will emerge.

A more abundant state *can* be achieved for all.

But for now, for you individually to increase your abundance (for that is why most of you will be reading our words on this subject matter), you first have to *believe* you are worthy of it. You have to *believe* that you are worthy of a rich life, that everything can be yours. You have to *believe* that this is the truth. And this requires that you face and release any lies you have agreed to believe along the way, lies that are currently in your way and have backed up the belief that this is a "some people win, some people lose" world. As an energetic reset, the following brief exercise (deceptively simple and highly effective) will help you reclaim your innate worthiness.

Visionary Exercise: Abundant You

Sit comfortably and begin to relax. Take a few deep breaths, clearing any thoughts about your day.

Let your gaze soften and your eyes relax. As you move along, reading the following individual steps of this self-guided visualization, allow your eyes to close each time as you turn your focus inward.

In your mind's eye, see yourself standing ten feet ahead. You look peaceful, with your eyes closed, as you stand in an expansive, clear white space.

Now look at your clothing and see it as pure white.

Take a moment to consider how abundant your life is. Think of all you are grateful for, and now see that abundance symbolized as a hue that colors your white clothes. The first color that comes to mind is perfect.

If you chose gold, wonderful. And if you did not, see your clothing now slowly begin to turn a brilliant gold.

Hold this vision of yourself in gold clothing and, with your peripheral vision, begin to see other shades and hues all around you — flying through the air. Silvers. Bronzes. Deep reds. Deep purples. Deep yellows. They gravitate toward you and become absorbed by your gold clothing.

See the warmth that spreads across your face and throughout your whole being as you watch these colors pouring into you. See the smile on your face.

Allow this to continue for as many minutes as you wish. When you feel positively full, walk toward this abundant you, slowly but surely. Step-by-step, the closer you get, the more open your heart becomes. Take as long as you need.

When you reach this vision of you, step "into" yourself so that the energy of this abundant you becomes absorbed. Experience how that feels. Just breathe, notice, and thoroughly enjoy the feeling.

When you are ready, return to the world you know, the one of the earth.

This exercise can be repeated regularly, and the very feeling it will give to you will help reprogram your understanding of what you are entitled to. Through feeling, it will help bring to you all that you deserve.

YOU ARE ENTITLED TO BE A WINNER

Money is merely an object. Money only has the energy that people give to it. Do not make money a god, for then you worship something that is nothing. You only worship the thought patterns and beliefs of a society that mostly got it wrong about money. Money is merely an exchange system that people use. It is given in exchange for a product, an object, or someone's time. Money is actually nothing as a force on its own. It is merely a symbol. When you worship money, you are worshipping material wealth — and that is not a truth. Money is but a means to an end. People should not desire a basket full of money to sit in their bedroom, for what good is that?

It is difficult for us to be sufficiently clear with those who are learning about abundance, for our understanding of abundance is an open heart and a life lived and experienced fully. Your training in the world of man is so opposed to this understanding. It is so ingrained that finances are *the* important factor, that having material things is important. There are many who have understood this not to be true, but even those souls are mildly infected by this belief, for it is energetically surrounding most people on Earth on a daily basis.

But begin to allow yourself to let go of this idea of money as a god and identify what money really is. *It is nothing.* It is a symbol that has power in the material world, and it can be a key. But in and of itself, it is a nonentity.

So when manifesting, especially if you choose to consciously create your life experiences, do not simply focus on sums of money, for then you are manifesting emptiness. Bring to light and clarify the reasons why you would wish to have the money (bearing in mind that a personal aircraft to travel around the world is not very likely to be that important to your development, so it is not likely to be manifested). Manifest true things — those things that will support your work, your life, your love. They *can* be manifested.

Like many, you may have a deep tie to this world of win-lose comparison and may deeply identify as being one of the people who lose. It is important to know that a change of mind can shift your role in this dynamic. So, right now, as you are reading this page, truly ask yourself, *Do I believe I am a winner or loser in the abundance stakes?*

All of you are entitled to be winners, to believe that winning is your entitlement — *entitlement* in the most positive sense of the word. For those who believe that losing is your entitlement, that will be your experience — that will be what you create. So become acutely aware of this. Look at your own un-abundant beliefs. Look at where you will not give to yourself in your life because of your outlook. Look at where you choose to make it harder than it needs to be.

DOES STRUGGLING WITH MONEY GIVE YOU A SENSE OF PURPOSE?

So many people enjoy the difficulty around money. It becomes a reason to live. Struggling to pay rent or struggling to find money to go on a trip becomes a guiding purpose for many. It takes a great deal of energy, *which is not necessary*, yet many people enjoy this way of being.

Therefore, become more honest with yourself about who you are in this equation. Do you enjoy the struggle? If your answer is no, yet you find you are often engaged in a struggle, then there is likely to be a part of you that feeds off the struggle. Is it the victim within you? And is it a role that you happily continue to act out? Or is it a karmic purpose at this time?

AFFIRMING THE TRUTH

You are entitled to everything. Whether you achieve it in this lifetime is irrelevant, but you are entitled to everything.

Affirmations are very powerful. If you think that you are one of life's victims where abundance is concerned, simply uttering the words "I am entitled to everything" can help shift your beliefs. Commit to saying this affirmation at least once a day and begin to notice the positive changes. It will help you experience more abundance and remove any limits you have wrongly imposed on what you deserve, on what you believe you are entitled to experience in this life.

"I am entitled to everything."

Do not compromise on *one* area. Many are abundant in love but not in work, or vice versa. There need be no trade-off. Understand that now. And if a trade-off is taking place in your life, a part of your belief system is allowing this to be the truth. It may also be that the time simply is not right for you to experience such abundance. Without speaking directly to you as an individual, we cannot identify whether this applies to you specifically, but we can speak in general terms. The prevailing belief shared by so many human beings is that it must be one or the other, that compromise is unavoidable. That is not the case.

Meditation: Abundance = Wholeheartedness

Imagine yourself now living the life you wish for, where everything is in place — your love; your work; your finances; your relationship with this world, with the people around you, with nature and the earth. How does that feel?

Again, close your eyes and imagine this experience.

See the fullness all around you. How does that feel?

Practice this as a daily meditation, accessing this feeling of wholeness, of wholeheartedness. For the more you access this feeling, the more you will bring it toward you as a daily reality. The more you meditate, the higher your consciousness and the more permanent your state of deeper connection becomes. Consciously focusing on the abundance within your heart and soul works in the same way.

If you are regularly accessing this feeling of your life being fully abundant, then you are carrying that energy with you wherever you go. That is the key. Without knowing you individually, we cannot entirely discern who needs such reprogramming and who does not. So if it feels true to you to do this exercise, go ahead and use it for as many days as you wish. It will greatly enhance the experience of your life and the abundance of your life. Truly.

THE EARTH IS A HEALER

Remember, too, that you will not always know what abundance is. You will have *ideas* — again, based on man's beliefs, such as the current belief that abundance on this planet means money and status and love (the appreciation of love is a good thing, of course). But planet Earth itself, and humanity's relationship with it, is all too often discounted. That is an important part of your abundant inheritance as well and must not be ignored. For when your relationship with nature is ignored, you become out of balance.

Nature rebalances man. That is what it is there for. This is the earth that you were born into. It is important to look upon the "face" of the earth, so to speak — and regularly — to experience its power. Those who deny themselves this aspect of abundance, who do not acknowledge this part of their being human, cut a piece of their own abundance away. And this denial affects all other areas.

The earth is alive, and it will help you open up. It will help you silently heal in the way you vitally need to be healed. Use the abundance of the earth. If we were a marketing team living in your time, our pitch to you would be "It costs nothing." You do not have to pay to visit the earth. It is all around you, and it will give to you if you allow it to. It will open your heart, and it will remind you that its beauty, wonder, and magic are all aspects of *your* abundance — your abundant inheritance.

APPRECIATION IS THE BEGINNING OF LIMITLESSNESS

Trust that practice brings you abundance. Spiritual abundance is a wonderful example. The more that souls practice raising their consciousness through whatever methods they choose, the greater the results. The results are visible. It works with any area of your life that you wish to make more abundant. Simply practice.

If it is love you are wishing to invoke in your life, as a true experience of heightened intimacy, then *practice* loving. Practice loving more. Practice being openhearted with those around you.

Animals and children are a wonderful help with this purity of practice, for they are less wounded and resistant, and they hold that openness, that simplicity. They are reminders of the heart and how its motivation is enough. And any moment when you truly acknowledge your heart, that is all that is needed to experience joy (*which you always have access to*).

On many levels, there is much more available to you than you are currently experiencing, and it is all too easy to throw in the towel, to be upset by the lack in your life. The truth is that when you begin to appreciate what you do have, then the universe will send you more. When you truly appreciate the wealth you have in your life right now — be it the people, your work, the roof over your head — then you have surrendered. You have surrendered to the already existent abundance around you.

And then there are no limits.

For when you surrender, you are too busy *experiencing* to build limits. The truth is that *there are no limits*. You *do* create your own reality. If you hold your vision and keep affirming to the universe that which you want, it will listen. You will manifest what you want. You will bring it to you that much quicker, even if it means accelerating those lessons that may be in the way of your desire. So be prepared. Ask and you shall receive.

STEP INTO THE FLOW OF GIVING AND RECEIVING

The one big truth in this is that *all* people deserve more, just as this planet deserves more from its people. And the only limits are the ones that are subscribed to and agreed to by the people. So watch your mind and watch the workings of the minds of others, and begin to decide for yourself on the abundant reality you choose to subscribe to.

Use daily techniques and affirmations. The ones we are giving would be a good starting point, but you can create your own. Use these energetic guidelines and intentions to show the universe what kind of abundance you wish to bring your way. And do not be ashamed of bringing riches your way — be they riches of love, of joyful experiences, or of the material plane and all that it has to offer. For if you are prepared to share your riches, you will create a flow of giving in your life that will always come back to you in whatever form necessary.

It is a beautiful truth that what you give out, you receive. So keep on giving. Keep on opening your heart to those around you. And keep on surrendering. And all the while, set your intentions for the life you wish to create. For abundance *is* your true inheritance.

Abundance Exercise and Affirmation

When it comes to abundance, are there areas of your life that are not quite going the way you thought they would? Did you set off in one direction, believing that things would fall into place, yet find that your goals and dreams aren't unfolding according to plan?

From the perspective of consciousness, an external lack of abundance is simply mirroring those areas where you do not give to yourself. You are generous with other people in so many ways, and now it is time to begin receiving all that you deserve.

Start by acknowledging and honoring yourself. Write a list of everything you *love* about yourself. Write at least fifty things and do it all in one sitting. Focus on aspects of your personality; your essence; your body; the skills, talents, and gifts you have; and any other qualities of being or doing that come to mind.

Some resistance may come up as you are making your list. At around the thirty mark, your heart might get a little tight. You may "run out" of attributes and want to stop. *Keep going.*

Once you have made your list, write the following brief letter of affirmation to yourself on a separate piece of paper:

> *I am fully deserving of wonderful abundance*
> *and joy in my life,*
> *and I receive that from the universe on all levels.*
> *Now and forever.*
> *For abundance is my divine right as a soul.*

Either keep this piece of paper on you at all times or display it somewhere visible to you in your home. Every day for the next two months, read this out loud to yourself at least once, if not more often. (If you forget a day, it's no great disaster. But if you forget a few days in a row, you must start the exercise over again and continue on to complete your two months.)

This is what we could call a "blasting exercise," as it will blast through the blocks you have to giving to yourself. You will see changes. And you may want to continue with the affirmation a while longer or even modify it to attract abundance in more specific areas.

Finally, trust the process of manifesting abundance. In addition to raising your overall awareness of abundance in your own life, an affirmation practice like the preceding one is a great and worthy technique that truly works.

CHAPTER 5

LOVING MONEY

❧

O ver a number of years of working with individuals and groups, I've seen how money is a deeply emotional issue for so many people. When, in 2009, it came time to create an online broadcast on the subject, "Loving Money" felt like the perfect title — an antidote to the fear, judgment, and general angst tied up with our relationships to money.

In my own life, at the personal and professional levels, I discovered early on that, really, there is nothing to fear about money. When we address it with openness and honesty, stress and fear quickly dissipate. In adapting the recording of the "Loving Money" channel for this book, I hope that the insights offered here will bring about a transformation around money for you — shifting your perceptions and showing you that it is truly your friend.

Money is an energy currency that is physically represented by banknotes, coins, and plastic cards — all means of circulating (giving and receiving) it throughout your world. In other words, money is an extension of your energy — both your personal energy and your collective or societal energy. And, as we will explore together, your energy is strongly influenced by your thoughts, beliefs, emotions, and experiences.

Society sees money as one of the great keys to happiness. At least, that is what the societal mind would have you believe. The societal heart is quite different. It, too, is seeking healing and freedom. You seek to understand more about money at a time when the world has a great deal of fear around it — fear of having it stolen, fear of losing it by your own missteps, fear of misusing it, fear of others having more than their fair share. Money concerns every person unless they are one of the rare few who live in a culture or situation where the currency of money is not important or nonexistent. At every level of consciousness, from the individual to the collective, the fear attached to money is an invitation to remember your empowered self.

Not having money and having money are both highly motivating and activating, in different ways. Fear and limitation ultimately wind you back around to parts of yourself that you are destined to be reunited with — you as generator, you as creator, you as lover of the world who is wired to give and receive in an abundant universe.

A great deal of anguish and pain arise within people because they give much of their power away to money. Money is powerful, but *you* are more powerful. Understand that.

Money is your mirror. When your money is tallied — when the numbers are added up, subtracted, and divided — you are seeing a reflection of where you are in your life. You play this game with the physical form of money. You review the numbers on your computer screen or the piece of paper showing your bank balance, and it is reliably representative of what you financially believe about yourself. In this regard, money is a key to your self-development.

It is good to see yourself where money is concerned. Your money energy flows in and out of you every day, and it needs to be considered. It is a barometer, giving you readings with regard to how good you are feeling about very important matters — about how you are using your energy, time, and other resources; about what you are bringing toward you; and about what you are giving and not giving.

Money invisibly affects and informs the kingdom you call your own. For example, if your kingdom is a one-bedroom apartment, you use your money not only to pay the rent or mortgage but also to decorate the space, to prepare meals in the kitchen that you may feed to others, and to share experiences with people you care about. However, people do not look at that apartment and see dollar signs. They see an expression of you.

You are expressing yourself with money all the time. You are creating with money all the time. Understanding that, you can look and see where the areas of limitation and freedom are for you in relation to expression and creation.

If you are experiencing hard times, do not be afraid. If you have a difficult relationship with money in this moment, it does not indicate a permanent situation or state of being. Money holds within it the perfect limitations and the perfect freedoms for any given moment in your life.

Below the level of conscious awareness, some people keep themselves at a scarce money level for an extended period when they feel they may learn something that would be for their highest benefit. We would say that there is nothing to learn, but there *is* something to *open* — something inside your heart. Money is always an invitation to extend compassion, kindness, and generosity to yourself — as you will experience in the following pages.

It is true what has been said: money is not everything. Money brings you certain experiences — and experience is everything. The experience of being alive is of the highest value. But "money" and "experience" get mistaken for one another and are often given the same value. They are not the same. And you run into all sorts of trouble (there are many who crash and burn), because, of course, only after great effort and striving do you realize that money alone cannot guarantee the experience — the felt experience — of being fully alive.

MONEY AND EMOTIONS

Money is an emotional topic for human beings — one of the most highly emotionally charged, as you may have noticed. In short, when you deal with money, you deal with emotions. Understanding this is one of the keys to mastering all energy.

Think about some of the times you have been highly emotional about money.

Has money ever worried or scared you? Has money excited and delighted you?

You have had a relationship with money all your life, even if it has changed many times over. Have you had a good relationship with it overall — uplifting, healthy, and supported by clear boundaries? Have you had a conflicted relationship with it — marked by low earnings, debt, struggle, and scarcity?

It is good to ask yourself questions such as these. They allow you to connect with the depths of your fears and the heights of your visions.

Through your explorations, we wish for you to connect with the knowledge that you have within you a *love* for money. You have partnered with this energy — the energy of money — to learn and grow by leaps and bounds. And if you are not feeling that love right now, don't worry. You will warm up to it before you are on to the next chapter and subject.

Making Room for Joy: Acknowledging Anger, Rage, and Helplessness about Money

Are you experiencing a lack of money at this moment in your life? Is money the object you are focusing on, to which you are attributing your lack of safety, support, or love? Is it currently representing all that is wrong? If you answer *yes* to some or all of these questions, how are you talking to yourself and treating yourself in relation to your situation? Are you motivated and looking for new solutions, or are you beating yourself up?

When you experience lack, "money joy" is not present. It's difficult to access positive feelings about money when it is seen as the thing keeping you prisoner in a situation of "not enough."

Beating yourself up over money is one of the surest ways to limit your abundance. If you are in a pattern or habit of being angry at yourself, your situation, or the world for not giving you the money you need or feel you deserve, you can move through that anger by exploring it. Just go into it.

Feel as helpless as it renders you, if that is where it takes you.

Feel the rage, if that is stirring within you.

Feel the fear, if you sense that you are in its grip.

Feel the weight of being a victim where money is concerned, if you relate to that energetic state.

Every emotion interacts with various parts of you in specific ways and is therefore different for every individual. Although you all share the same spectrum of emotions, the experience of any given emotion manifests uniquely inside each of you.

Whatever feelings are present for you, allow yourself to *feel* them. Feeling is one of your greatest healing capacities. You cannot be angry for long when you visit the anger. It is when you skirt around the edges of the anger, afraid to let it erupt because of the sadness underneath, that it can take longer to clear.

Also, do not feel alone in the emotions that money evokes. If you don't feel safe, for example, remember that many do not feel safe right now because the energy of change is moving so fast. Those who are most deeply asleep are feeling the most unsafe. Money provides an excellent focus for this. You will likely relate to this on a personal level. Everybody has experienced fear around their money situation, now or in the past.

The Money Mind and the Money Heart

We have begun to explore your feelings toward money as it stands in your life right now. And then there are the thoughts, ideas, and opinions you hold about money. Those are quite different. They come from the mind. A feeling comes from the body and the heart.

This brings us a little closer to the heart of our discussion — acknowledging the *money mind* and the *money heart.* So often these two remain unaligned and seemingly at war with one another.

This battle, frequently waged without conscious awareness, is one of the great difficulties if you are rapidly evolving spiritually yet still struggle with old money wounds. Money memories are deeply ingrained in both the human psyche and also the energy body. There are strong ancestral patterns around money. Added to which the majority of people do not have as much as they would like. That has been the template that has been running. Through this conversation and the exercises woven into it, your money heart and money mind will begin to come into alignment with greater ease.

You can rewire your money energy very fast.

Addressing the raw emotional force of money, and taking responsibility for your thoughts about money, will make this so.

Let's take a brief moment to look within at your money ceiling at this particular time.

Inquiry Exercise: How Much Money Are You Ready For?

Imagine that you were given $100,000 or €100,000 tomorrow. How would that feel?

Truly feel it for a few seconds.

If that feels good to you and there is no hesitation or fear, multiply the amount by ten and now see what sensation you get in your body. Imagine receiving $1 million or €1 million tomorrow. How does that feel to your body?

What would change in your reality due to that influx of money? How do you feel about those potential changes? Are you ready for change?

Now, ask yourself, *How much money am I ready for?* Even if you have no specific goal in mind or need for more money at the moment, let yourself see and feel the amount of money that you are ready for in your life right now.

Write down that amount on a piece of paper. And write down a few words to describe how that amount feels in your body.

How did that inquiry feel? If the amounts discussed felt uncomfortable in any way or made you a little nervous when you considered the impact they might have on your life, that insight is key. If you felt comfortable, good. And if you felt uncomfortable, it is important for you to start considering why you would feel uncomfortable receiving all that money.

Often this ties in with your sense of deserving and worthiness. You might mistakenly believe that you can *do things* in order to deserve more or to ensure your worthiness. But in truth, you are inherently worthy and deserving — simply because you exist. You are worthy and deserving because you are an expression of divine love. You are worthy and deserving because your courageous heart beats.

No monetary value could be put on you. That is one of the real reasons why money is seen through the lens of lack. There is not enough money in all the world to represent the value of one human life. So "How much money are you worth?" is a preposterous question. *Net worth* is simply an unfortunate turn of phrase because of the way it gets misconstrued and internalized by people.

However, the money and other resources that come to you often reflect the way you value yourself. It is that mirroring effect again. Money goes where valuing flows. Sometimes, focusing purely on loving and valuing yourself can turn finances around, without any consideration for money.

So, we will underscore the difference between *being* valuable and valuing yourself. They are not the same thing. And then there is the difference between *being* worthy and determining the value and worth of something, such as the amount of money that can be exchanged for your time, skill, expertise, or mastery.

Understanding and always remembering the difference between "being" and "doing" will serve you well.

You are often figuring out ways to value what you *do* and what you *give* — all separate from who you *are*. You negotiate hourly rates, yearly salaries, flat fees, commission percentages, and royalties on revenues received. Determining the value you offer is entirely up to you and can become increasingly easier and more enjoyable as your understanding of money grows.

APPRECIATION: THE DOORWAY TO TRUE ABUNDANCE

At its heart, money represents appreciation, both toward yourself and toward others. When you pull your paycheck or client payment from your mailbox and take it to the bank, you can view it through the eyes of love and see it as a way to appreciate how you have collaborated with others and participated in the world through your own contribution. Do you find it difficult to embrace your earnings with a happy heart? If so, do you know what stands in your way?

The simple act of tipping is a good example of appreciating others. When you tip waitstaff, a taxicab driver, or the one who cuts your hair, this is a way to say "thank you." It is an act of respect — gratitude made tangible for a service you have received — and a very interesting moment of choice, for there are no concrete rules here. Tipping is optional for the most part, so you are able to see how you feel about the extension of money to others. Do you find it difficult to give your money away? If so, what are you afraid you will lose? What are you afraid will not be returned to you?

These are simply questions to ask yourself. Whatever your conclusion is, celebrate it! Do not be discouraged, even if the conclusion is disappointing. If you discover a part of yourself that has limited capacity where money is concerned, this is good. You have found an area of limit inside you, and now you can move past it. An area of limit does not have to be permanent, even if previous experience has instilled doubt. You already know this, but it is good to be reminded. Awareness awakens you to more of your own power. And even if you have struggled repeatedly with the same issues and the same areas in your life, you are moving through and beyond those old limitations now.

If you are experiencing lack, allow yourself to look beyond your bank account and your debts for a while and notice everything — the opportunities, the support, the friendship, the love — that does come to you regardless of your bank tally. When you feel appreciation for what is, you are energetically inviting more abundance of all kinds.

If you are already experiencing great abundance and ease with money in this moment, appreciation for all the money that has come your way — and the work, gifts, and other channels through which the money arrived — is a very healing emotional state. Gratitude for, and clarity about, the money you currently have further opens you to the many gifts you have received in your life.

Most who read this book are privileged to be in situations where money flows in a far freer way than it does for some of your fellow brothers and sisters in the world. To notice and be aware of this is to tune the dial of your attention to appreciation. The energy of appreciation is one of the most powerful forces on your planet — powerful enough to end poverty consciousness. This is because appreciation *frees* you.

It is a brave and generous emotional state because it's unabashed in its spontaneous acknowledgment of another.

When made a priority in the day-to-day living of your life, appreciation quickens your evolutionary journey. In the future, your world may come to be a place where there is no longer a need for physical money in your giving and receiving — not because there has been total financial collapse, but because you will discover more refined ways to exchange energy and resources.

꩜ ꩜ ꩜

As we move through these layers of conversation on money, notice what you feel now.

Do you feel a little tired? If so, that is all good and well. We are moving through fields of thoughts and feelings to see what catches, pings, or releases for you.

If you are feeling uncomfortable, you can open up again by simply placing the palm of your hand on the center of your heart chakra. As you do that, supporting your heart physically, allow yourself to open to more of what is going on within you.

Because your heart is needed to lead your mind and intuition, it benefits greatly from the comfort of your touch. The safe boundary of physical support helps dissipate anxiety and over-thinking and allows the energies of love and possibility to rise.

Exercise of Breath and Light: Loving Money

The following exercise is helpful when you feel anxious about money or are experiencing any low-vibration feeling around money.

Take a deep breath in, and as you exhale, breathe out any thoughts or feelings that you no longer want inside you. Breathe out anything that feels limited or difficult, even if you do not fully understand why it feels that way.

Then take another deep breath, and as you do, think of all the thoughts, feelings, and moments from your past involving money that you would like to release from your being. Let them go...breathe them out.

As you are inhaling and exhaling, you may wish to visualize a circular opening where your crown chakra resides. See a funnel connected to the top of your head, allowing a cascade of gold-flecked white light to come down from above. The gold light represents the currency of money, and the white light represents your eternal connection to a universe that will always bring you what you need.

As you release past limitations through your exhalation, you are filling yourself with the money energy of the now. This money energy is yours.

Breathe in, then breathe out — receiving and releasing, receiving and releasing.

From this open and peaceful place, can you love the money that allowed your parents to feed and clothe you before you were even aware of this currency? If you felt deprived, can you love the money that did come your way during childhood?

Can you love the life your money is currently helping you live? Your home, however small or large? Your mode of transportation? The places you gain access to? The people you are able to gather with?

Open your heart to money and it will open itself to you. Now, feel yourself continuing to be filled with this cylinder of gold-speckled white light from above. Feel it warming you, filling you with new money energy.

You may repeat this exercise as often as you wish. It is perfect for removing blocks to the energy of money.

You attract to you what you are resonating with. If you encounter a day or a time when a familiar situation is becoming uncomfortable, move yourself emotionally out of that state of vibration to help increase your money flow. Move toward anything that gives rise to your exuberance, enthusiasm, and curiosity.

When you are consumed by negative emotions and humming at a low vibration, it is difficult to attract high vibrations and energies to you. When your life slows way down or seemingly stops because you hit depression or another emotional wall, if you remain in that energy for a long time, your money energy can become unsupported. Sometimes, this is perfect. That situation may suit what it is that you want to learn or experience.

If you resonate with what we're saying, it is also your responsibility to remember that you have this ability to choose your resonance, because it will absolutely be your medicine in those moments.

And why not give yourself the medicine? Why give yourself a difficult experience of money rather than the antidote that can bring you back to balance?

Many of you give yourself a difficult experience of money out of loyalty to the mass consciousness, loyalty to your human family who has suffered through all kinds of poverty. However, as you open more to appreciating and loving money — and as you become increasingly better equipped to give more — blind loyalty gives way to a dynamic new mode of connecting with your world and the people you share it with.

Old patterns of feeling trapped or wounded around money are able to disappear. Eventually, they will no longer be a part of the landscape of your days.

Visualization: Walking Your Money Path

We will close with a brief energetic exercise to increase your experience of "money love" for the next twelve months. After that, you should be up and running by yourself —

enjoying the energy of money, and money itself, with greater ease and flow.

With a soft gaze, allow your mind to rest, and *feel* your body internally. What do you feel physically right now? Do you feel calm? Do you feel restless? Beyond the thoughts you are thinking, what sensations and emotions are you *feeling*?

Once you are tuned in to how you are feeling, in your mind's eye, see a path ahead of you. This is no ordinary path. It is an electric-green, luminous path that starts at your feet and runs straight to infinity. You can't see the end. It just disappears into the distance. This is your money path for the next twelve months.

Have a closer look at it. What is the path like relative to your feet? Does it feel wide enough to you? If it doesn't, go ahead and widen it. You are not looking to broaden it in order to increase the amount of money you have. It is about being comfortable on your path of money. So make it as wide as you would like.

Now imagine that you are moving along this radiant green path. Are you walking? Gliding? How are you experiencing your movement? The energy of your body is moving downward through your feet and into this path. Your energy is meeting your money path and giving it all the necessary information to understand your currency needs and desires. Your energy holds what you need financially on the soul level *and* the human level — both of equal importance.

As the information circuit between your energy and your money path begins firing, let it show you what your *golden sum of money* is — your ultimate sum. What is the golden amount sufficient for you to realize your dreams? Allow yourself to see that sum of money. And as you see it, *feel* it as well.

If the sum you chose surprises you, or if it is different from the amount you would typically opt for, go with what you have chosen now in the moment. This sum is the truth of the moment.

How does your golden sum break down? What amount of money would you be satisfied with each year? What amount of money would you be satisfied with each month? And what amount of money would you be satisfied with each week?

Now, as you continue moving along your money path, pick a number between 0 and 100.

The number you have picked is the percentage of your money energy that is currently focused in the past. There is no great drama if you chose a high number. This could work in your favor if your past was more financially abundant than your present. Let's break it down by decade and see what your relationship with money was like — what your overall experience of money was and how you felt.

- What was your experience of money when you were a child, up to ten years old?
- What was your connection with money like when you were an adolescent, eleven to twenty years old?
- What was your connection with money like when you were a young adult, twenty-one to thirty years old?
- If it applies to you, what was your connection with money like when you were thirty-one to forty years old?

- And what about forty-one to fifty years old?
- Fifty-one to sixty years old?
- Sixty-one to seventy years old...and beyond?

If you have feelings flooding back into you, breathe them out if they are uncomfortable. Do not be alarmed. It is an achievement to *feel*, and it signals that you are ready to release something from the past.

Now focus your attention on your feet again, looking at your money path and sensing the movement ahead.

See something very small yet bright glinting in the distance. You can glimpse it straight ahead of you. It is as if rays of light are bursting through to reach you.

Stop moving and allow yourself to observe this glowing, bright light up ahead on your money path. It may appear as a gold light. Or a bright white light. Or maybe it appears as a multicolored spectrum of energy...bursting through like a fireworks display.

Allow this light to come to you. It could take a while; it might not be instantaneous. It may have a fair distance to travel to reach you, but allow it to move toward you.

As it gets closer to you, notice how your path begins to change color as it meets this energy.

This powerful light — multicolored, gold, or white — is getting closer and closer until it is almost touching your skin. This is the *sun* of your money energy. This warming light, which is now either directly in front of you or safely enveloping you, is the beating heart of your money energy. Feel it. Feel its life. Feel its color. Feel it giving to you. Feel it filling your body.

When you feel fully nourished by this energy, allow it to start slowly retreating, fading to a pinpoint in the distance, until it finally disappears.

Remember that you can access this special light anytime you would like to or need to. As you step off your money path, know that your twelve-month money transformation has begun.

If you struggled to bring your money energy close enough to you, repeat the exercise until it gets closer and closer. And see this as a moment of triumph, because you have identified another blocked area that you can now release.

This exercise involved *receiving* and *releasing* at the same time. You saw your golden sum of money. And you saw how much of your money energy is focused on and connected to the past. You received an abundance of positive energy and new possibilities. And you released the energy of emotions related to money that may have been keeping you stuck. This is the key with money energy — *to understand that the flow of money is circular, not linear.* It is not a straight line. The flow of money is a circle of plenty. As you give money, so, too, do you receive it. And as you receive money, you find countless way to release it — using it for living your life and sharing it with others.

In the joy of receiving money, and in the beauty of giving money, may you experience ever-expanding money love.

The Money Affirmation

My relationship with money is full of ease and grace.
I listen to what it is saying to me.
I pay attention to what it is showing me.
I value how it helps me grow.
Money is a reliable mirror, reflecting my energy
back to me each day.
Thank you, money, for being my transformational friend.

CHAPTER 6

SLEEP

A Surprising Key to Self-Mastery

---

*T*he core energy running through "Sleep: A Surprising Key to Self-Mastery" is one of knowing the self beyond the body and beyond what we perceive the physical to be. It is a real reminder of the presence of spirit in daily life.

Presented here is the idea that we wake up every morning, and it's the birth of new possibilities. It is a new day. We can begin again. When I first channeled this material, in January 2009, it resonated strongly with me, and it does so more all the time. It gave me a new understanding of the renewal properties of sleep and how essential it is as the time when we resolve situations and concerns and energetically reset.

It also gave me a new appreciation for the power of napping! I used to see napping as unnecessary, but now I have room inside myself to slow down, relax, and think: Maybe a nap would be good right now. I appreciate that scientific studies support this, confirming the benefits of twenty- to thirty-minute naps for our energy levels.

Until recently, sleep was a largely unacknowledged part

of our lives. It was something we just "did." But now we're
collectively coming to the understanding that sleep is vitally
important on every level — physically, mentally, emotion-
ally, and spiritually. What this conversation showed me is
that not only can we overcome obstacles to sleeping well,
but we can become masters of this nightly renewal process.

Understanding and mastering sleep is a great lesson, for when you
learn to master your sleep, you learn to master yourself. Are you
someone who sleeps with ease or someone who has great difficulty
with your sleep patterns? If the latter, have you done everything
you can to address that difficulty? Have you looked at potential
nutritional deficiencies or hormonal imbalances? Do you perhaps need to sleep alone yet still share a bed with your partner
because you do not want to upset them? Have you considered giving yourself permission to sleep separately, realizing that it might
be what you need? (Self-permission alone can release some of
the tension in any situation, sometimes in ways that change your
energy enough such that no further action is needed.) The sleep
remedies that will specifically serve and support you will become
clearer as your understanding of sleep expands.

So let's begin by exploring what sleep is.

Sleep is the process of letting your body rest. You close your
eyes and enter a different world until at a certain moment something wakes you back into your body. But what is the deeper
purpose of sleep, and what are the opportunities within it? Sleep
is known to regenerate your physical body — your cellular body.
The sympathetic nervous system gets to slow down. The muscu-
lature gets to rebuild. The organ systems get to rest.

But what is sleep beyond this? What does it mean for a human
to be asleep? Where does the mind go? Where do the emotions
go? Do they all go to sleep, too? No, they do not. They do not

need to sleep. The *physical* energy body sleeps, yes. But the soul does not, and your mind and heart are the points where your soul most strongly connects to your human identity. This is why sleep is so important, for in this state the mind and heart rhythms are in complete harmony — in sync for the nightly healing journey.

The experience of sleep is unique to every individual. Energetically, you leave your body in sleep, yes. You remain connected to some degree, but the rewiring of your mind and body is done by a force other than you: your oversoul — the connector between your human self and Higher Self.

Entering into the sleep state is to surrender to a kind of death. You allow the human you to "die," usually for anywhere between four and ten hours, depending on how long you like to sleep. In effect, you disappear from this physical form, just like in death. The only energetic difference between a corpse and a sleeping person is a pulse.

SLEEPING, DREAMING, AND RELEASING PAST-LIFE WOUNDS

It is important to look closely at how those who have disturbed sleep are not in the full sleep state. They are somewhat in between. Why? Sometimes it is because they are stuck in a past-life time line. Those who have recurring, difficult dreams or even tormented dreams — where they wake in fear or anxiety or sweats — are often people who are poised to awaken more fully in consciousness. And these dreams will be one of the keys to awakening for them, as a means of solving a past-life wound that has been, symbolically, a "knife in time" that they haven't known how to release.

People who live with this kind of torment are very tired, usually on many levels — physically, mentally, emotionally, creatively.

And the tiredness is good, for they need to be tired of these old energy wounds in their lives in order to dissolve them. They need to get to the end of their tether. They need to get so physically sleep-deprived, or so distraught by the recurrent anxiety, that they are compelled to investigate and uproot the cause of their depletion.

For those who deny the investigation of such an experience, the cost can be high. They may deny themselves the freedom of their hearts, for they will not feel safe. They may not feel safe around other people. They may not even feel safe to be on the planet. Paradoxically, for human beings who have a very difficult life and do not know how they will keep going, sleep is the answer.

It is not just for the physical rest. During sleep you heal yourself of wounds gathered over the course of that day — emotional, energetic, and psychological wounds. Sometimes an event during your waking hours will trigger a past-life wound so subtle that you are not consciously aware of it, but during the sleep state this triggered wound, which has moved into your energy field, is seen and dissolved, gently probed until the energy disperses.

THE POWER OF LETTING GO AND ALLOWING

Those leading the way in consciousness are already more open-hearted and willing to grow in this lifetime than any previous lifetime. If you are incarnate now and heading into enlightenment, you are likely having the greatest experience you have ever had as a human being.

But this is also why you can be hard on yourself about your blocks and areas of resistance. It is a little like kicking yourself when you are inches from the finish line of a great race. It is like saying to yourself, *I did not do well enough* — but without seeing that the very fact that you are identifying something that has held you back is an extraordinary achievement. This tendency is another reason why sleep is your ally.

The sleep state rewires you. No matter what you have been through on any given day, it brings you back to a centered place of being. Think of the deepest moments of grief in your life and how hard it was to move through those times with an open heart or any sense of love or joy. Your system simply could not have withstood the experience of enormous grief without being supported by the regeneration properties that sleep brings to your soul.

Sleep gives space to all your feelings. It brings clarity to all your learning.

It births the forward direction latent inside you — with the fullness of heart and vision you want. This is why some of you have dreams of foresight. You are the visionaries who have psychic dreams, ones that show you a future pathway and something to come. Whereas others of you often have past-life dreams but do not recognize them as such.

If you are someone who has wonderful dreams but does not remember them when you wake, how freeing this can be! How freeing for your mind that you have no need to remember the details. Sleep is the part of your life that you do not get to see the details of. Isn't that a fascinating way of looking at it? For some of you, a whole third of your day is hidden from view. There is nothing you are missing, though. Sleep is not about seeing. It is about experiencing. It's about allowing. It's about resolving. Sleep brings you back to a greater understanding of your life. It offers an expansive perspective that adds to the feeling of freedom. It is the moment of "zooming out," if you like, whereas being awake is when you are "zoomed in."

While sleeping, you die, in a way, to your human self, and you return to the highest point of source reached on Earth while still connected to a human body.

How do you feel about that information?

You may be greatly excited and joyous. You may feel unsure. You might feel fear. And none are likely to be the reaction you expected — and that is part of the process of mastery. When you reach mastery tests, it all becomes a lot *less* clear to your mind. Emotions feel more random. They follow fewer logical patterns. That is because there is no map for mastery. You only need to get to the starting gate of your mastery journey — and begin. From there, the universe will arrange itself around you accordingly, providing an abundance of signs, signals, and synchronicities to support your journey.

SLEEP AS YOUR NIGHTLY HEALING REMEDY

If you are looking for ways to remedy what ails your body, ease your mind, and heal yourself on various levels, it is time for you to start giving yourself the help you need. If you are ready to play with journeying during your sleep, know that you can command the direction of your sleep if you are not getting what you need during your waking hours.

Exercise: Requesting an Energetic Shift

Remedy for the Day

Before you fall asleep, say aloud or in your mind what energy it is you feel you need as a remedy for the day: "I need the energy of trust," or "Kindness toward myself is the energy that I wish to be bathed in during my sleep tonight."

If you are feeling frustrated or angry, you do not need to know the specific remedy. You can simply say, "I feel frustrated. Please move that energy during sleep." Or "I feel stressed, and I ask that my sleep help me release this stress." By directing attention toward a specific energy in this manner, you *will* experience transformational healing — and powered at two to three times greater strength than if you had not made this request.

Remedy for the Physical-Emotional Pain Connection

If you are experiencing fatigue or are managing a chronic illness, before you go to sleep, state the emotional or mental components that are adding to your pain (for instance, sadness, worry, frustration, jealousy) and then request what you need more of — more confidence, more happiness, more peace, more fun, more trust, or more faith, for example. An example sentence might look like: "During sleep tonight I wish to let go of worry and frustration about my physical health. And I invite more support, trust, and love energy to aid my physical healing and well-being, right now."

Once you have acknowledged and stated both aspects, let it all go and go to sleep.

Apply these energy remedies every night if you wish. And do not be shy about doing one or more of them many nights in a row. The only consequence if you do them every night is that you will speed up your progress. That is all — for you are not asking for a particular manifestation in this state. You are simply asking for the kind of remedy known as an energetic shift. And when you open to the remedy, you receive it — day and night. Many of you go through a tortured journey when awake because you forget to ask for the energetic support that is readily available. Remember to ask. Ask for what you need.

CREATING A SACRED ENVIRONMENT FOR SLEEP

The mastery of sleep is to know what sleeping conditions you need and recognize the sacredness of those conditions. For example, if you are experiencing insomnia, creating a sleep-chamber environment using certain scents, sounds, or mood lighting can help promote well-being, supporting your nervous system to relax and surrender into sleep. Not using electronic devices or being in stimulating environments a few hours before you sleep will also help with this.

If you are protesting that you do not have time to recognize the sacredness of sleep right now, that's okay. See and know that. Acknowledge that right now you may be prioritizing busyness over sacredness, for you think the two cannot coexist. And yet, sacredness creates the space for soul-led *doings*. Human busyness simply perpetuates more busyness. There is a difference. There is no busyness in sleep, but there is great doing *and* great undoing. There is great revealing and great releasing. There are great fears and great joys. There is great learning and great loving. There is the possibility for everything within sleep. So take time to examine the sacredness of your sleep chamber.

YOUR LIFELONG FRIEND

Those who have vivid dreams may believe that the images are the strongest part, but when the story is vivid, it means that feeling is operating at the highest level. And you have to understand that dreams *feel* big and vast, for they do not take place in your mind. They are not restricted to the limits of that physically sourced faculty of the human body. Dreams emanate from and are projected throughout your whole energy field, so they are wide in scope and vibrationally alive.

Some dreams initiate processes and put things in motion for

you. For example, one evening you may dream about love, and that is the catalyst for the realization that you are ready for partnership. And over a period of three to six months, you are inspired to get yourself more and more ready for love's arrival. Other dreams may resolve things for you or give you clues to what is going on in a specific part of your life. And some may give you the emotional tonic you need for rebalancing and healing. Those going through loss, grief, or great fear, where sleep is the only place love is felt at high levels, are often surrounded by angelic beings waiting to be invited to bring their support. More help is given to these individuals through their sleep than at any other time.

So remember this: help will always find you, and sleep is a way to receive it.

Sleep is your friend. It is your ally. It is rejuvenating and regenerating and readying you for the next day. Every single night when you go to sleep, you release the past. And depending on how good at releasing the past you have become (how willing and how open to change you are), sleep becomes a fast track of the awakening process. You may feel tired when you wake up because you are doing a lot of inner work during sleep. If this resonates with you, know that it is a sign of success, for it means you have started to accelerate your rate of release — release of the past and any corresponding patterns of limitation.

Upon waking each day, you are returned to the wonders of the earth and all that is felt, seen, and experienced here. In sleep, you are returned to the wonders of the world inside. The world that is bigger than your physical body. The world for which your physical body is the central point of focus in this grand life experience you are having.

If you are one who is psychic and occasionally have psychic experiences at night that frighten you, the fastest way to remedy this is to commit to your psychic experiences in the day and study what is coming through you. "Study" means whatever seems right to you. It may simply be a commitment to self-observation, or it might involve going to a workshop, reading a book, or keeping a journal of your extrasensory experiences.

～ ～ ～

Not surprisingly, the best time to sleep if you want to have the broadest energetic experience is when the majority of people sleep, especially if you live in a densely populated area. The collective energy quiets down and becomes lighter. Less density is felt when you walk around a city when people are asleep, for example. That is because there is less involvement of the human ego and physical body at that time. On the other hand, this is precisely why individuals such as Lee find it such a joy to stay awake in the middle of the night and create, or just *be*, for there is so much space energetically.

Do you like being awake at night, too? Do you enjoy it when the world is quiet? What does the spaciousness give to you, or in what ways does it inspire you?

YOUR CONSCIOUS CONNECTION TO SLEEP

As we come to the end of this conversation, once again look at what a healing experience sleep can be for you. Recognize what freedom the journey of sleep can provide. And remember the power of stating your energy remedies before you sleep.

Love yourself through your sleep. So many have challenges of the heart when stepping into self-mastery. If you are one who is having challenges, sleep will be the answer. This, we can assure you. If you are one who is opening to the understanding of how energy shifts work, start talking to yourself before you sleep and create your energy remedies. It is extraordinary what you can reconfigure by consciously directing your attention in sleep. If you are experiencing something difficult or painful, are you willing to surrender it to sleep? Could you possibly allow sleep to solve something for you, something that you have been struggling with from all angles or trying to release? Why not offer it to sleep?

✧ ✧ ✧

Take some time to reflect upon the key moments that arose for you during this conversation. Even if the concepts are not brand-new to you, the energy of what these words mean to you can spark positive and even profound change. You may have created a new doorway into a world of self-healing that will accelerate your prosperity, growth, happiness, and health, or deepen your sense of connectedness to everything, including the heart of humanity. When you connect to the heart of *you*, it cannot be otherwise.

Sleep is a key to your heart. Use that key. Use it to unlock whatever dreams and desires you wish to unlock. The space of sleep is created for your transformation and regeneration. Harness that knowing. Feel safe in that knowing. And begin to celebrate and enjoy your sleep again — perhaps more deeply than ever before.

The Sleep Affirmation
Sleep is a healer of my body, mind, and soul.

Standing on the shores of sleep each night,
I gently release any and all limitations
into the ocean of consciousness.
And I am softly bathed in the exact energy remedy
I need in the moment —
even if I'm not consciously aware of what that remedy is.

Sleep is my faithful friend.

CHAPTER 7

THE EYE OF AWARENESS

*T*aking place in Stroud, England, in May 2007, "The *Eye of Awareness*" was one of the first public channeling sessions I did. I remember feeling that the unique focus on awareness offered by the Zs had enormous potency for helping people open psychically and access a visionary state sourced from spirit — and the potency remains true. One of the primary intentions of this channel is to support people to not get lost in the physical, 3-D reality that we're immersed in each day. At this time, there is so much fear of the future that many of us are quite crippled when it comes to looking ahead — whether on a global scale or at our own personal hopes and dreams. But we very much need to befriend the future. We need to activate the gift of foresight so that we can care for the future with awareness and vision. The following discussion and the energy contained within it provide an illuminating way to do that.

We are very excited to be here and to speak with you of the *Eye of Awareness* — a conversation and a realization that can change your perspective forever. The topic of awareness is addressed in depth in the fields of meditation, mindfulness, and spiritual development and is seen as a key part of the evolution of consciousness. Awareness is one of your greatest allies in evolution, for when you are equipped with awareness, you can see into and through anything you encounter, both internally and externally. You can cut through any emotional or mental binding; you can free yourself from any prison, energetic or otherwise. In this way, awareness serves you on your journey into your greater power.

The Eye of Awareness is a profound component of the larger story of awareness. It is not a simple matter to describe it in words, but we enjoy the challenge and promise to make it quite understandable.

The Eye is both an energy and an entity. It is the life force that drives consciousness; therefore it contains great power. It exists in the universe, just as your body exists, just as your spirit exists (tangibly and intangibly), yet it is known and understood by very few. The Eye of Awareness is an energetic faculty that allows you to fully and deeply see — with far greater insight, understanding, and clarity — what is occurring around you. It allows you to see beyond the physical and beyond your initial perceptions of people, places, and experiences.

The Eye expands your vision and also allows a greater influx of light into your energy field so that you can see more clearly. Imagine for a moment that you are walking through a moonlit forest. You can see silhouettes and shapes, you can see the outline of trees, but you walk tentatively, knowing that you could easily stumble along the path. You could trip on a rock, or walk into a tree you didn't see coming, and it would probably hurt a bit. *I need more light,* you say to yourself. *A flashlight, a lantern, a way to see what lies ahead.* Your daily life is much the same. You need more light in order to see clearly. The Eye of Awareness is an often untapped source of light that you can access at any time — one that will illuminate your vision and, as a result, upshift your experience of life.

ILLUMINATION: SHINING A LIGHT ON YOUR POWER TO CHOOSE

You have had moments, hours, days, weeks when you have felt illuminated within your being — full of light, full of wonder, full of inspiration, full of clear seeing. Imagine what the *next* level could be: a regular grounded presence of full clarity and sensory awareness, in every single moment. Illumination is one of the greatest functions of the Eye of Awareness. When light is brought to the dark, you stumble less. Getting "knocked off your feet" — by another person, by an event, or by some misstep of your own — happens less frequently. The Eye brings to the forefront awareness that you previously had not been able to meet or to absorb vibrationally, but now you can.

Illumination strengthens and amplifies your ability to choose. It turns your moonlit forest into a sun-filled forest. And when you have joined with the Eye and activated its power in your life (as you will do shortly in a visualization), while you might still stumble into a tree or two initially because it can take time to reprogram habitual movements and interactions, the Eye will show you the greater choices available to you — those that were previously hidden in the shadows.

The power of choice is greatly underestimated on Earth. You have the ability to think, to feel, to contemplate, and to reason, but your entire reality shifts based on your power of choice. *Choice is the turning point.* And in that sense, choice is a magical power. Therefore, the Eye of Awareness working in your life, and showing you the multiple choices available, can change everything in an instant. Whether it happens today, tomorrow, or next week, anything you wish to change *can* change if you are willing to see your choices and decide among them.

You must first experience the Eye of Awareness in order to begin to understand it. In the following visualization, we will describe it to you, but you will also have your own images and feelings arise — and that will be perfect.

Visualization: Activating the Eye of Awareness

Part I: Opening Up to Expanded Awareness

Imagine the sun that you see every day above you, giving light and life to your planet, fueling your life cycles. The Eye of Awareness is much like your physical sun. It illuminates everything you experience, fueling your spiritual life cycles.

See this sphere above you — the Eye. Allow it to take on whatever shape and color it does for you, knowing that your interpretation is correct for you. It may look to you like a physical eye. It may look like a golden orb or an iridescent portal. However it appears first, take a minute to see the extraordinary amount of light it holds. This light is pouring down onto you, bathing all the elements of your life in its luminous rays. See it gently illuminating you, the people around you, the animals, your home — everything — with its brilliance. Notice how they transform into higher, more loving, illuminated versions of themselves as this takes place.

Now turn your attention to how the Eye illuminates your heart. The Eye is not a mental concept or construct. The quality of expanded awareness it generates in your inner senses is *real*. Some think of awareness as a mental faculty. In truth, awareness is an energy-based capacity that is most nurtured and fed by the heart. Allow yourself to feel this awareness-heart connection within you. Allow the Eye to illuminate your heart for a moment, as you sit and allow the light in. Then, when you are ready, you can bring your focus back to our words on this page.

The Eye of Awareness is connected to you from above through your spine — through the back of your physical and energetic body. If you are familiar with the chakra system, the subtle energy centers located in and around your body, see a golden thread connecting each of your chakras to the Eye of Awareness and its vast power. If you are not familiar with chakras, simply see a golden thread running along your spinal column, connecting you to the Eye — this conscious light being.

The reason the Eye is connected through and along the spine is for the purpose of facilitating your energetic coherence. Awareness expands when you are centered. When you are not centered in your energy — when you are overstimulated in one area or emotion, or leaning forward in your energy field to interact with others or to race through your life — you are off-center. Turn your attention to the Eye for a minute or two, and feel yourself come back to center.

Part II: Resolving Conflict through Expanded Awareness

Now, using your inner vision, see the people in your life, especially those who surround you at your home, in your workplace, and in your friendship circles. Allow the light emanating from the Eye of Awareness to bathe them in its radiant warmth, giving you a clear view of each person in their highest, most authentic state of being.

Now, think of a person with whom you are having conflict, whether minor or major. See that person standing ahead of you in your mind's eye while you maintain your connection to the Eye of Awareness. What is the conflict about? What are you struggling with? How is the conflict affecting your life?

Allow the light to brighten around the other person so you can see who they truly are — with their emotional body, personality, physical form, and spirit revealed in great detail and sharp focus. How is the conflict affecting *their* life?

Allow the Eye, with its ability to cut through confusion and stuck thoughts and emotions, to shed new light on the issue or challenge that lies between you. What do you see? What do you sense? What do you feel? You may want to write down some of the information you become aware of.

Using the Eye in this way, you may experience an immediate release, a freeing up of your energy. You may see a different way to approach this problem or a new choice that was previously obscured from view. Take your time. There is no need to rush this process. Simply recognize that when you are focused on your connection to this spiritual sun — the Eye of Awareness — your intuitive and spiritual vision is twenty-twenty. From this vantage point, what is possible for the two of you in the future?

Allow yourself to feel your connection to awareness itself. It is solid. You can count on it. When you are in the dark —

confused or feeling mired in negativity — desirable options can seem limited or even impossible to come by. With spiritual awareness, new options appear in abundance. And when you see these options, you feel the exhilaration that comes from having choices. You feel the joy of empowerment, knowing that you can move forward.

Take a moment to allow the Eye to fade from your inner vision, but knowing that it is always there for you. From now on, you carry it with you everywhere you go, and you can access its powers of observation and insight whenever you choose. In times of conflict or struggle — with people, with circumstances, with yourself — remember the Eye. It will always amplify the pressure-release apparatus within you, and you will feel the pressure dissipate. The relief that comes from having clarity is a great healing force. The Eye is yours to connect with, as it is a part of you.

CONSCIOUS CHANGE:
MOVING ELEGANTLY BEYOND LIMITATIONS

Wherever you are on your spiritual journey, and however long you have been pursuing personal growth, there is one core fact from which you cannot escape: *awareness is the precursor to conscious change.*

There are changes that occur in your life that you do not choose, which then allow your awareness to grow. For example, the death or loss of a loved one can profoundly change your perspective and your life overnight. But let's look at the other side of the coin, where awareness is the precursor for conscious change.

As your awareness grows, you will begin to look at your life differently, at situations and relationships you have created. You see the multifaceted nature of your creations. You see the lessons, layers, and nuances. You see the cycles and patterns. You see the positive and negative potential outcomes. You see the deeper meaning of things...and much more. And it is your increasing awareness that allows you to see the changes you wish to make. In other words, expanded awareness *creates* change. Without awareness, conscious change cannot occur.

When you consciously make changes, it is because you have decided that something needs changing, usually because it isn't working. The most common experience for people, as they begin to awaken and deepen in themselves, is to find that difficulties arise whose cause they cannot assign to anything on the outside. For example, both your personal and professional lives may be quite happy and fulfilling, but inside you is a yearning. This yearning is your deeper awareness tapping you on the shoulder and giving you the proverbial wake-up call. The question, then, is: will you answer the call?

Awareness Illuminates All — from Limitations to Possibilities

Awareness as a spiritual opening can be challenging to navigate when the expansion begins. As you grow and cultivate a wider awareness of yourself and your life, you open the door to new possibilities. Once you begin to open spiritually to who you are, it can be a deeply rewarding yet difficult path to follow, in large part because as your awareness of your new possibilities grows, suddenly the limitations you have created for yourself cannot be ignored.

Imagine, for example, that you are a schoolteacher and have realized that you no longer want to be, even though you have valued empowering children through their learning. Instead you want to write books that will empower people in a different way.

You have secretly *always* wanted to be an author. Do you remember what blocked this dream? Perhaps the fear of what your parents would think, what your teachers would think, or not having enough money or security. Teaching seemed to offer greater certainty. But now your awareness of your deeper desire is growing, and you see that you have bound yourself into a contract for the next year or two with your school, and this limitation feels difficult. Awareness is showing you the big picture: the exciting new possibilities, the stifling limitations, and the choices to be made.

The common response is to become disheartened or feel disempowered because you see that you have created a complicated trap for yourself. However, that is not the truth. There is always a way for everything to work out. But first you may have to contend with the idea that you will let people down or hurt them; that may be a belief you bought into long ago that holds you back and keeps your vision at bay. It is far too easy to stay trapped in relationships, duties to others, and service roles that have ceased to serve *you*. And if something is not serving you anymore, you can bet your life that you are not serving the people you think you are, either.

Imagine you run your own business, and someone works for you who really doesn't want to be there any longer. Would you want them to stay? Would your concern about not finding a willing and capable replacement outweigh your desire to find someone who truly wants to work with you? This is an important question to answer honestly, because if you would rather they stayed, it signals that you are dealing with fear. In the ultimate reality you can create for yourself, you would not want to indenture someone who really does not want to be in your employ.

Exposing the Inner Judge

As your awareness grows, your inner judge will be more and more visible to you. Go back for a moment to the example of you as the schoolteacher whose dream of becoming an author is resurfacing, and see how the inner judge appears in that scenario. As you become aware that you have other options, your inner judge is likely to say things to you such as, *You can't let the children down. What would your students and the other teachers do if you weren't there? What would the administration do? For them, you are a rock of stability.*

Yes, maybe you are a rock to the school, but the school will find other rocks.

Don't be misled. The inner judge is a great deceiver because for many years it has been bending the truth in an effort to keep you "safe and sound." And maybe right up until now it was exactly what you needed. But there comes a time to break the codependency with certain aspects of self that you have grown beyond.

Think about it for a moment. For you to make your way to this new world of possibilities there will be some things from the world you are currently in — activities, behaviors, dynamics — that you will have to leave behind. This need not be dramatic, like big sweeping changes in your relationships or your profession. It could just be certain ways of being or certain parts of you that are ready to be retired. There is a world within you — archetypal forces and many aspects of self. You see yourself as an individual human being with a name, with a particular personality, but you are not a one-dimensional being. Think of how you are able to move through different states of being. There is the you that is happy, the you that is optimistic, the you that is pessimistic, the you that is depressed, the you that is in love, the you that is searching for something, and the you that believes you have found something.

As you begin to open more to who you are in truth, in your heart and in your soul, the many energies and archetypes within you are free to change according to your real needs and wants

— according to your *current* needs and wants. Some of these energies will die, and many will be born. And you will gain more than you will lose through this process.

It can be painful on the spiritual path when you are confronted by a side of yourself that you do not like. For example, you may repeatedly crash into the inner judge we spoke of or one of its cohorts, like the inner critic. You have a few days when you feel elated, and then to your dismay, you begin to listen to some harsh inner dialogue. Suddenly you're feeling frustrated, irritated, fatigued, or depressed again.

But take heart. As you meet these sides of yourself that you do not enjoy or believe to be you anymore with greater awareness, know that positive change is in motion. Begin by just *meeting* these parts of you. When they arise, call on the Eye of Awareness to see these aspects of yourself, but without responding to them right away. Just allow them to be (allowing them to be is quite different from allowing them to act out and create drama).

Simply begin to notice the part of you that shifts from happiness to fear. Notice the fear itself. It came from within, so there is no need to be afraid of it. It may have been triggered by something or someone outside you — by your employer, your oldest friend, even your beloved partner — but these are just triggers. The situation, circumstances, or people are not the feelings you are experiencing.

This is a crucial distinction to keep in your awareness, because these feelings will come up over time. The *you* that is growing and expanding will essentially ask you to purge. That is what the opening of awareness does. You have achieved this awakening through many steps, stages, and years of work — the work of spiritual vigilance. Awareness relies on your spiritual vigilance. Every single day that you are alive is an opportunity to observe yourself and grow by doing so. You will not always enjoy what you see, but when you see something you *don't* enjoy, you can ask it what it has to teach you and then release it. Practice allowing yourself to not react to it, to not try to flee from it. Just notice it. See it. Observe it.

When you begin this journey back to your true, liberated self, you will find many things you will want to change as you are observing and sensing and feeling more. Do not put any pressure on yourself. If today you suddenly become aware that your life is not how you want it to be, that is not a tragedy. It is a gift, because you have seen something you did not see before. You have seen the next chapter of your journey.

TRANSMUTING FEAR

Yes, at some point you will choose to let go of certain aspects of your life — relationships, career paths, creative projects, spiritual pursuits that you are currently following. You have probably already let go many times in your life. If you haven't already done so, make your peace with letting go in order to *gain*. Even though fear of letting go is one of the great spiritual battles for those who want to change or to create something new, it can be transmuted. You can pull the anchors of the past and be free to sail on. The Eye of Awareness will help you identify and let go of your anchors — as many as you wish. The illumination of the Eye allows old energies to dissolve far faster than if they are not present in your consciousness.

The question is: are you willing to pack your bags and go traveling, metaphorically or literally? Understandably, human beings are most afraid of what they do not know. When you face your fears, you often realize that you were generating more fear around an event or person than was actually necessary. In truth, you have an extraordinary ability to let go of attachments to people and places. When you look directly into your heart, you know that the love won't disappear; only the attachment and dependency can be dissolved, and that typically takes time — allowing you to adjust to the changes.

We invite you to embrace change. Do not fight it. Do not grieve long for those parts of you that have done their work and are no longer needed. Recognize that as certain energies and archetypes are disappearing, new archetypes possessed of a higher consciousness are arriving — and these are archetypes you will adore.

IF THINGS ARE HARD RIGHT NOW

If life is difficult or depressing for you, if it currently feels as if you are surrounded by too many locked doors, your growing awareness is going to help you. It is going to help you see the blocks, see how to release them, and see the ways forward. Trust this.

As your awareness grows, you will have more psychic and intuitive experiences. You may already have a strong intuition. Imagine how it could be if it were even stronger. Imagine if you were tapped into a source of knowing, of peace, of love that never left you, that was present and available all the time. How beautiful would that be? You deserve to have that experience, and with the growth of your awareness, you will.

As your intuitive awareness grows, you will find yourself hungry for more contact with people like you. That will be important. It will help you understand who you are more quickly and easily. It will help you grow faster. You will be able to tune in to the thoughts and the feelings of others, which will cause you to be more discerning when it comes to choosing whom to spend time with. If you walk into a room with a group of negative people, it will be harder for you to stay with those people for long because their energy will be overwhelming. As you cultivate this greater awareness, you may initially find yourself needing to withdraw from certain people. If that happens, do not be afraid. Once you are well on your way along this journey into deeper awareness, you will find yourself able to be centered in the most difficult of circumstances. You will know where your center is — a home within you that you did not know you had.

COMING HOME TO THE INFINITE YOU

You may be in the grip of deep awakening right now — awakening to who you came to this earth to be, recognizing that you are infinitely powerful and that there is infinite love within you.

You are stripping away some of the aspects of self that would interfere with the steadiness of the infinite you. You are brave in your willingness to see these parts of yourself and to allow them to go. You may be one who works tirelessly on this purging process without recognizing what you are doing. What you are doing is *extraordinary*. It requires great courage and spirit. You are giving yourself freedom rather than staying trapped in fear.

You have drawn to yourself the keys to freedom, and we are honored to be one of the resources through which you find your freedom. You are the most important person — the most important being — in your world. If you are a parent or deeply in love with your partner, this will be difficult for you to understand. However, as you access deeper love for yourself, the love for others will multiply tenfold inside you. Imagine that. Think of your dearest loved ones now and imagine being able to love them far more than you already do. This is where the Eye of Awareness is leading you, not only back to yourself but deeper into love with others. It is your portal to this love.

And how will all this come about? Through the power of your greater awareness. You have done your spiritual research and work. And you are using the knowledge you have gathered over the years to apply your awareness. Like a skilled automotive engineer, you have learned how to take your engine apart, investigate its workings, and put it all back together so that your vehicle is attuned to the frequency you wish it to be attuned to, a *higher* frequency.

Everything you do where spirituality is concerned is a way of remembering yourself. Everything you are working on now will come to fruition. If you do not feel that you have yet found your place, you will. There is a place in this world for all that you are. Whether with another being or on your own, whatever you are trying to find that you have not yet brought to light — it is already here...and it is looking for you, too. Focus on the Eye of Awareness and you will see. Try the visualization exercise daily for a week or two, and start to notice the changes in your vision, your feelings, and your life.

The Awareness Affirmation

I turn toward the Eye of Awareness,
the conscious light of clarity that is my powerful ally.
I open to this radiant light that penetrates
all confusion and darkness,
illuminating the path to my highest good
and greatest experience of life.

CHAPTER 8

SEX AND SEXUAL ENERGY

B ecause so many people experience blocks to their sexual energy and sexual expression, causing far too much frustration and suffering, I hosted a live online class on this topic in 2008. The Zs and I joined forces to offer healing perspectives and pathways to reconnect to the sexual self. At the heart of it all, I believe that to reconnect with our sexual energy is to reconnect with our personal power. Not surprisingly, the recorded version of "Sex and Sexual Energy" quickly became one of our most popular audio programs. This chapter is adapted from a segment led by the Zs, one part of the larger conversation that reflects the healing message of the whole.

As energy masters, you are artists whose palettes consist of many forms of energy — physical energy, mental energy, emotional energy, spiritual energy, and love energy, to name only a few. Sexual energy is one form of energy around which there are many sensitivities and misunderstandings. We will take a few steps here toward clarity so that you may fully enjoy and make good use of this brilliant, empowering, and healing vibration.

Sexual energy is your life-force energy, and many of you are suddenly opening wider to this energy within yourselves because you want to accelerate your process of awakening. Sexual energy is your creative energy, the well from which feeling, being, doing, and achieving spring forth. It is the well of life's magic, bubbling with aliveness and possibilities.

As a field of energy, it is running all the time, and how you choose to use it varies greatly. Sexual energy for so many in your world is invoked through your work — through your physical work, your intellectual work, your innovations, and your collaborations. Wherever passion gives birth to something new, you know that sexual energy is in play. As human beings, you can certainly see this in your prolific creative expression, including your works of art.

Sexual energy as life-force energy permeates everything in your physical world. Sex itself is only one stream of its boundless expression. It is also expressed as the aliveness that you share with friends and family members. Sexual energy is an aspect of the hugs and laughter and lightness that you give and receive. With healthy energetic boundaries in place, you don't need to shy away from this. It is an important part of the spark and sparkle of life.

Your sexual energy acts as a radar, signaling you when there is a strong resonance with others, whether it be with close colleagues, friends, lovers, soul mates, or a different type of connection. Once you recognize and feel the attraction that you have to other beings in your life, of whatever nature, you will start to see the alchemy occurring — the coming together of unique elements that brings something new into the world.

FEAR AND MYSTERY SURROUNDING SEX AND SEXUAL ENERGY

Some people secretly wish they were more sexually "open." They hold ideas or pictures in their minds about what being sexual or sexy looks like and then determine that they don't look that way. Each of you observes and absorbs so much of what surrounds you — so many different ways of expressing sexual energy and sexual behavior in your family, your community, your society, your world. In your developmental years, you see representations of sexuality and try to mold yourselves accordingly — so that you will be accepted, approved of, wanted, needed, and loved. You begin to be influenced by these external representations of sexuality from your earliest days. The beliefs and attitudes, the hopes and dreams, the fear and confusion — it all begins in childhood.

Sexual energy is the energy from which you were born. When children exhibit high levels of sexual energy, they are simply expressing the life force inherent within them. This can horrify some parents, for they do not know what to do with this behavior if they grew up in a society that advised them to hide their sexual energy and keep their sexual behaviors a secret.

You are probably not a stranger to the embarrassment, shame, and fear that many children take with them into adulthood. Tied into those feelings, a shroud of mystery around sex and sexual energy complicates this beautiful and elemental force.

It's time to shed some light on the matter.

Awareness is always a powerful way to initiate positive change, so let's take a moment to look within and see what you came to believe and feel when you were young.

Awareness Exercise: Uncovering Sexual Beliefs

Take a slow, deep breath to connect with yourself.

Breathe in again…and breathe out.

Take a moment and think about the region where you were born, grew up, or spent the majority of your childhood. If you moved around a lot, pick the one that you felt had the most influence on you.

When you were growing up, what were the cultural attitudes toward sex? You may remember news headlines or magazine covers focused on this topic. How did you feel when you saw them?

What did your teachers and other people in authority in your community convey about sex?

What were the messages you received, verbally and non-verbally, from your parents or guardians regarding sex and sexual energy?

Take another deep breath…and release it.

If you have siblings, what messages did they knowingly or unknowingly convey to you about sex?

And what about the other kids around you — neighbors, classmates at school, and your closest friends? What did you learn about sex from them?

Let yourself see, sense, hear, or feel the beliefs and attitudes that you adopted.

What were your first impressions and experiences of sex and sexual energy throughout your formative years?

What aspects of sex felt safe to you?

What parts of it felt unsafe?

Now, gently place your hands facedown, with one palm on your stomach and one on your heart. You may want to hold your hands still or softly rub those centers in a circular motion. If you're having an energetic or emotional reaction, just allow it, while staying present with yourself.

Acknowledge yourself for your willingness and courage to look back in time, no matter how often you have done so before. As an energy master, you know that there is always value in tending to your emotional world.

If you are ready to release the limiting beliefs and feelings that you inherited — these first understandings — while retaining all the positive ones, affirm this to yourself.

With your next out-breath, release what you no longer want to believe about sex and sexuality.

With your next in-breath, inhale the enlivening and healing essence of sexual energy and sexuality.

Once again, breathe out the limitations. And breathe in freedom and joy about sex and sexual energy, even if you aren't completely sure what that looks like or how it feels at this moment.

You see, dear ones, the fear and mystery were not coming from inside you, after all, as so many of you have believed. They were passed along to you by those delivering the messages. They were experiencing their own fears around the topic and were busy weaving their own web of self-protection for managing this strong and sometimes frightening energy.

Incarnation is a wisely made choice, and with great pre-planning you choose your family of origin and the other people surrounding you in your early life. There is no mistake, and this is important to remember so that you may find compassion for yourself and those who have played significant roles in your evolution as a human being, especially when emotional pain has been a big part of your shared story.

Many people emerge from childhood and adolescence with very low expectations of sex. Some go into sexual experiences just hoping they won't get hurt, emotionally or otherwise. And so when it doesn't hurt them, but it also doesn't give them enormous pleasure, they settle for that. Measured by that scale, it feels like a success, because what they were in fear of (that is, getting hurt) did not manifest. They experience relief from the fear, and — without consciously knowing they are doing so — decide that "relief" is good enough.

FREEDOM FROM THE SEXUAL WOUND

Beyond those who simply settle for mediocrity (which is very painful, indeed), many people are in a serious battle with their sexual energy — and their sexual selves. This manifests in varied and nuanced ways, but some of the common battles are:

- shame about one's appetite for sex (whether it be a strong appetite or minimal);
- shame about experiences that happened in the past, from innuendo and teasing on one end of the spectrum to assault and rape on the other end;
- shame and self-loathing about one's sexual identity,

especially if it's outside of the accepted norms, such as being bisexual, homosexual, or transsexual; and

• embarrassment and shame about one's sexual desires if they are outside culturally accepted bounds, such as a desire for nonmonogamy, a.k.a. polyamory, or to explore other aspects of sexuality considered alternative or "kinky."

If you are experiencing conflict in this area of sex and sexual energy to any degree, you are not alone. This would describe the majority of human beings. There is much fear of being exposed, rejected, and unloved.

But you have suffered long enough.

If you have long believed that you are "wounded" sexually, do not label your experience that way anymore, for it will not help you. In order to see the rapid progression and healing that is possible for you, allow yourself to acknowledge that your sexual past is truly not unusual. You may have felt isolated and terribly alone in some of these experiences, but in truth, countless other people understand and empathize with what you have gone through.

Also, replaying emotions that were too difficult to process in the past — "re-feeling" them now for the sake of your growth — can be very tiring for an energy body. If this is true for you, know that the recognition and remembrance that you are not alone can be so healing that you may never need to revisit those shame-based emotions again.

Yes, there are some who have only ever had positive, healing experiences of sex and sexual energy. But the majority have experienced significant shame, and this shame comes directly from *judgment*. So, if you want to release your shame the fast way, release your judgment — and your shame will disappear automatically.

In fact, if you have shame about anything you have experienced in your past, notice what stands out most clearly for you right now, and ask yourself:

- What judgments do I have about myself and about this situation?
- What judgments do I have about words I spoke or actions I took?

We ask that you not view any past sexual experiences as mistakes, for that would mean heaping more judgment on events and encounters that were probably very vulnerable experiences in the first place. Do you see how that becomes a vicious circle? That is the addiction to the wound. It is fine to play out the pattern as long as you need to for your growth. But there comes a point where both the wound and the pattern can *disappear*.

That is because understanding, forgiveness, and love are far greater and stronger than shame.

LIFE AFTER SHAME

Know that you can breathe easy from now on. Your past sexual experiences no longer need to hold you back or prevent you from pursuing the new experiences around this energy that can arise for you — be they through intimate physical connection, creativity, productivity, new dimensions of communication and self-expression, or simply opening to greater pleasure and enjoyment of your physical life on Earth. Whatever form these experiences will take, just know that *new* is ready for you. *Bigger* is ready for you. *Wider* is ready for you.

New, bigger, and *wider* can mean more peace and spaciousness around your sexual energy, more emotional freedom where sex is concerned, or a more spiritual experience of sex. It will change in the ways that most suit your energy, your unique circumstances, and your evolving life path.

THE SACREDNESS OF SEX

Sex is often referred to as being "sacred." This is because when you open to this energy, you open to the energy of life itself. You open to oneness. You open to the joy of creation. And touching the sacred in yourself and another is why sex is so compelling.

Again, your sexual energy is healing energy, and that capacity is also an aspect of the sacred. And so even if you had deeply hurt feelings about sex in the past, you may find yourself becoming much more interested in it as you open up and awaken. Your sexual energy is the furnace that burns away the heavier energies from the past — the anger, resentment, blame, fear, and pain.

A fundamental truth is that no one can give you the ultimate experience sexually if you are not open to receiving it, which often starts with giving the ultimate experience to yourself. The willingness to explore your own physical body, to know your desire energy body, and to love your sexual self changes your vibration. When you care for these amazing aspects of yourself, the radiance of your soul shines through your physical being — and that is very sexy, indeed.

That said, it's also true that there is an ebb and flow to sexual energy. You may lose interest in sex entirely for certain periods, such as in times of loss or great change, or during times of awakening when you're adjusting to the new and bigger energies. If you are struggling mightily to feel anything or to see a new vision for your sexual self, we invite you to be patient with yourself. Let it go for now. Do not push yourself. Do not struggle. Do not bang your head against the wall.

Just reach a hand toward this part of you. Call it forward. Welcome it home.

Remember that it is your vital life-force energy and is forever a part of you.

It is your *heart* in so many ways. And your heart energy rises when sexual energy is liberated to do its healing work in your life.

Although the expression of this energy will shift and change throughout your life, it will continue to be a fundamental part of your physical energetic experience on Earth — through acts of giving, nurturing, creating, and connecting; through experiences of enjoyment and pleasure; and through rejoicing in love's expression.

The key to unlocking the mysteries of sex and sexual energy is always love. For example, if you are stuck in sexual habits with a partner and you both would like to open to a new and wider range of experiences but are not sure how to, start by turning toward the love you share. The love you hold for each other is what inspires your desire to join together. It can also give you the courage to communicate more deeply and honestly, to talk about your needs and wants with a new level of vulnerability. Is there a sexual experience that you've been curious about but afraid to discuss? Is there a fantasy that would be exciting to talk about, even if you don't really want to enact it? Is there a technique you would like to explore or a workshop you've been secretly wanting to attend? This love will be the bridge between you as you speak from your heart.

THE HEIGHTS OF SEX AND SEXUAL ENERGY

Sex gets much attention in your world, as you have noticed. You sense its immense power even if that power is misunderstood. Let us be completely clear about its healing and awakening capacities....

It amplifies your energy to such a level that everything in you opens (your cells, your chakras, your heart), and distractions disappear. It takes you to realms of intimacy with yourself, another, and life that can change you — dimensions of closeness, tenderness, and oneness that dissolve the painful illusion of separation. It takes you to experiences of the heart that your mind cannot fathom.

These are some of the heights of sex and sexual energy — energetic experiences that words can only approximate. Know that there is nothing to fear at this high "elevation." There is peace here. You will not meet anything you would not like, for you are speaking about a pleasure energy, a joy energy.

And even if you are still feeling the impact of past traumas in this area, understand that your traumas are being released even as you read these words.

With the expansion of your sexual energy comes the release of fear. When fear disappears, you get a rush of energy through the body. That is what sexual energy does. It rushes energy through your body so it is flush with happiness. And that happiness can transmute old wounds, fractured relationships, and bad memories.

This once-conflicted part of your life experience — your sex and sexual energy — can now be rediscovered as medicine for your body, mind, heart, and soul.

What may have felt like a dark and damaged part of you can now be rediscovered as beautiful, powerful, and whole.

The Sacred Fire Affirmation

My sexual energy is fuel for my life.
It moves me into action. It inspires me to create.
It infuses me with the courage to go
where my heart longs to go.

As a physical manifestation of this energy,
sex is my sacred friend —
giving me glimpses of home,
welcoming me back into the arms of oneness.

CHAPTER 9

THE ESSENCE OF SUCCESSFUL RELATIONSHIPS

Tapping Into the Energy of Trust

I delivered this talk in August 2008 to an audience of five hundred people — my largest public group at that time. The night before, I barely slept. My body was on fire, and I had many dreams about family members, friends, and other personal relationships. As is often the case, I didn't know in advance what the topic would be, but when I woke, it was clear to me that I had gone through my own fire journey, so I was curious about delivering this message — whatever it was going to be.

The atmosphere in the room after I had finished was very different than it was before I began. I remember noticing that strongly. Many people from the audience came up to talk with me afterward, several of whom were in tears. One man who had lost his wife the year before thanked and hugged me, and said he had experienced a healing around his grief during the channeling session. I was more than a little humbled and at a loss for words in this intimate moment with him. And I think it will always stay with me, reminding me of the power of this work to affect people deeply. The connection travels, whether it's across the room when I'm onstage, through the computer screen on Skype, or through headphones via an audio recording. And it was this event, and this lovely man's feedback specifically, that encouraged me to keep going with the work I do — and to trust that we reach the people we're meant to reach.

Welcome to all of you. Today we have come to speak on relationships, for that is so important at this time. We will look at one of the greatest influences on self-discovery: the choices you make within the relationships you have.

As many of you will already know, you are receiving the energy of everyone around you all the time. You are energetically merging and morphing: receiving what it is you wish to, rejecting what you don't, and letting go of anything that doesn't feel important to you.

From the moment you were born into your families and cultural groups, you started to receive from those around you. You started to shape yourselves based on how far those around you allowed you to go and how they encouraged you, but most importantly, who they were being energetically. For it is *who you are* as energy beings that people feel, not what you do. Who you are inside comes first — the frequency of your thoughts, beliefs, and feelings — and people sense this. When it comes to impact and response, what you do is secondary.

Recently, we said to Lee, "If you announce to some people that you are a spiritual being or a channeler, you may fear they will now think you are strange or weird." But we assured him that they already know that he is different, because they feel it. His describing the work he does in words is just the confirmation.

And this is the truth for all of you. This is how you read

each other. And that is why when you meet another soul you feel attracted to, you will be drawn to them based on their *energy*, whether you feel they will be in your life for just a moment or for a lifetime.

LOVING BEYOND TIME AND SPACE

First, let us implode one of the myths around relationships that humanity holds within its mental framework. It is the idea that any relationship with another human being must last forever to be of high value, or higher than those short relationships you may have. This is not the truth, so please let it go. Let that knowing be a part of the healing release, if you are one who has experienced the loss of people in your life, whether because they exited this plane or because the two of you came to a place of discord, separated, and went off in different directions. The number of days, months, or years you shared together was the truth for both of you at that time.

The reason why this can be so difficult is that when you join your love with another being, you place your investment in your love with *them*. An energy of love, created between the two of you, is nourishing and feeding both of you. So, when that person suddenly disappears or walks away, or when you feel *you* have to walk away from them, it is one of the hardest losses human beings experience — particularly for awakened or sensitive beings. You feel the removal of an energy from your life, an energy you want back, and this can be painful.

But understand this: there is no one in your life whom you have loved or who has loved you who has not sparked something off that was already inside you. To put it a different way, it is wonderful that another person helped you find and experience the love you have inside. You collaborated to experience love's growth within you, and if this person with whom you were in a relationship disappears, the love itself does not disappear from inside you.

But the pain of the loss can often make the love shrink to a very small seed in you, which may require reawakening.

A DEEPER UNDERSTANDING OF HEARTACHE, LOSS, AND LOVING OTHERS

Let's look at the human pattern of the soul-mate relationship or love relationship — that very close intimacy between partners. This type of partnership has a particular cycle. The human energy template in the less awakened form — and by this we mean those who are not conscious of their energy or spirit and believe only in the illusion of physical life — often goes through cycles of heartbreak where love is concerned. Many people use heartbreak to open further to life and to love, but they do not know this, which is why it is so painful. The pain is increased because they do not see the release occurring inside them.

Release is necessary for growth, because space is needed for growth.

The truth that all of you share is that five to ten years from now, your life — especially your energy and your emotions — will not be the same. Trust that. Trust that you are always moving, and that is as it should be. And there are relationships that will come into your life that will serve you perfectly at the right moment.

If you are someone who is experiencing the joy of long-term relationships and long-term intimate friendships, it is wonderful that you have stability with others, shared histories you are forming, and opportunities for personal growth you did not imagine were possible. At the same time, it is important to keep letting go of history to allow the future to be brighter than the past.

RECONNECTING ENERGETICALLY

If you have experienced heavy grief and loss, we want to help bring some relief to your heart and soul. Remember that at any time you can energetically tune in to your connection with whomever you feel the loss of. It is important to understand that if you feel such loss and grief, reconnecting to them in this way will deliver to you everything you need if the exit was abrupt or if you weren't capable of feeling and experiencing the depth of your love for them when they were present in your life. For example, reconnecting with them energetically can give you the opportunity to express thoughts and feelings you have been holding within you.

You may have associated many other emotions with this loss, in addition to grief. You may harbor guilt, resentment, or some other conflict with certain people, but we ask you to put all that aside right now and go back to the love. The love will help burn through any of the difficult or painful emotions far faster than anything else.

Love is your great power. Oh yes. You are an extraordinary being. You have this incredible, multilayered energy system and emotional power structure inside you, but your love fuels the growth of your energy and power. That is why love feels so good. When you have lost someone or even when you fear loss, love more. Love bigger. Love deeper.

Let's do a brief exercise where you can share this love with someone you are missing and who is strongly in your awareness today. Connect to their energy and their heart.

Exercise: Connecting Energetically to the Heart of a Lost Love

Bring to mind someone in your life whom you feel you have lost. This could be someone who is alive or someone who has passed — no matter how much time has gone by since you were last together.

From the vantage point of today, see them anew — see who they truly are. They were the perfect person for you at the perfect time, and when the time was no longer right or had come to its natural end, they disappeared. And you disappeared from their path.

You have grown and plotted a different course because you have taken the seed of their love, their energy, and multiplied it. You have made it more diverse through your own unique forms of expression. Everything that they sponsored in you or gave to you is safely within you now.

Once again, with your inner vision, see this person ahead of you in your mind's eye. See how perfect their arrival into your life was and how perfect your experience with them was. Trust that while they are no longer physically in your life, they are forever in your heart and forever connected to you at a soul level.

In your own way, thank this one for the love they have shared with you.

Receiving the gifts that you two spirits have given to each other is an important step to take, not only on the path of healing but on the path of evolution. Why? We will explain.

You all absorb each other. You get near to another being, rub up against them energetically, and absorb little pieces of each other. It is not that you are taking from each other. *Absorbing* in this sense is opening in response to what is being demonstrated, shared, or given by another — much like the pores of a sponge opening to absorb water.

There was a time when Lee was quite fascinated by the kittens he raised. He was fascinated to watch one of them do something for the first time while the other one observed, and then the next day both kittens were able to do the new thing. Taking turns being in the lead, they both learned by following. This observational way of learning applies to observing other energies, too. You observe other energies, and, through seeing, feeling, and otherwise experiencing those energies, you are able to activate them inside yourself.

Take the example of a television program that holds a high resonance of love through the inspiring stories it depicts or by featuring someone very loving, such as Oprah Winfrey. You are likely to feel drawn to the people and the good feelings. If you are one who is using the power of your observing and seeing, you will be able to activate the love inside yourself in response to the program. It is the same within your everyday life, with your children, friends, colleagues, and all the people around you. You are energetically rubbing up against those you enjoy in order to find out who you are. That is why the more you awaken, the more important it is to consciously give yourself over to the good vibrations you feel around you, rather than the frequencies you experience as heavy, negative, or limiting to you.

The more you wake up, the more sensitive you become. The more sensitive you become to people around you, the more open you become to yourself, and vice versa. The more fine-tuned you become, the more readily the people in your life will start to change, if change is needed and agreed to. You will lead the way as you further develop the consciousness, awareness, and love inside yourself. And others will respond to this expansion in you.

This is not the story for everyone. Many of you have experienced rejection, people pulling away or sometimes attacking. This is because love is a force you are either ready for or not (even though love is your source — it's a great paradox). Similarly, every single individual on this earth holds within them the full potential to experience enlightenment, as you like to call it. That is without question. But attaining enlightenment will not be the choice all will make in this lifetime.

You must trust the choices of those around you as you wake up more and more. There will be some who do not want to go where you are going. If you are not the person to open their eyes or their hearts, they will know. They will feel it. So trust them. They will get whatever it is you want them to get at some point, in some way. It may not happen for them in the way you would like to see it happen, but that is when you have to trust the people and the relationships in your life.

It is important not to become what we would term a "love terrorist." This is someone who barrels through all boundaries and blasts another with their love — their focus, attention, affection, and more. When a person *wants* to be blasted with love, it is so good to have that big infusion of it. But if you are someone who is not looking for love or not ready for that level of intensity, then you will experience this as an invasion and will have to get away. Or shut down to the energy of love coming at you. It is all about individual desires, capacities, and boundaries.

Is there mutual desire and an open invitation to enter another's heart and life? If not — if there is resistance or fighting — there is terrorism. Terrorism is the slowest way to solve anything, for it is all about control and an idea you hold of somebody else that may or may not be true.

YOUR BELIEFS ABOUT OTHERS

Beliefs are ideas that you hold tightly to over time. They become your codes for living, and they must be examined if you want your close relationships to thrive. As you know, some beliefs become outmoded and limit your life experience. What you believe others think of you, what you believe others think of themselves, and what you believe to be true about other people's lives is rarely correct.

Even if you are deeply insightful about others, you cannot fully know another person. You cannot fully know every single part of them — what makes them tick, what their strongest commitments are, what their soul's intentions are for their life. You may experience the highest levels of consciousness and love with them and join with them in expansive ways. You may have the most extraordinary and joyous time with them. But will you ever fully know them? No. Knowing and understanding this is important for experiencing nonjudgment and compassion for another. If you truly understand this in your heart and not just your head, you give everyone space to be themselves — and this is one of the most generous gifts you can give another being.

There are those who have learned to give people the space to be themselves. They are the "love givers" rather than "love terrorists." If you identify with this, you have likely seen it as your role to give to everyone in your life. In time, you begin to understand that it is important to go with what authentically feels good to you instead of taking action based on a pattern and role of being a caregiver. Your giving arises naturally from the heart, bypassing the pattern in favor of something that brings real joy and happiness to you and the person on the receiving end of your love and care.

SEEING YOURSELF FULLY:
THE MIRROR OF RELATIONSHIP

The next stage of growth is to give space to yourself — emotional space, mental or psychic space, and, sometimes, physical space. This can be a tricky process involving all sorts of emotions you did not see coming. Why?

For one thing, as a "sensitive," you have absorbed a little bit of a lot of the energies around you. You have absorbed a little bit of your mother's pain and empathy, your father's anger and loneliness, your best friend's joy and fear, your sister's shame and ambition, your brother's anxiety and curiosity. Your reasons for partaking in these energies are pure. You wish to relate to them and understand who they are. Out of love, you want to energetically meet them. And, more importantly, you seek to find yourself through them — gathering up the many parts of yourself in the mirror of "the other."

As you begin to realize that you can be yourself with other people, you begin to release your attachments in certain relationships, as well as the emotions associated with those relationships that you no longer need. You get off the roller-coaster ride, where one minute you are fine and an hour later, out of the blue, you are feeling anger and irritability. These are sometimes feelings you have absorbed from another. The unquestioned belief is that if it is coming up and out of your energy body, this is *you*. But much of the time, you are releasing the energies of others.

If your emotions tend to fluctuate greatly, check in with yourself regularly throughout the day and ask yourself how you are feeling. If you hit a wall — a place of angst or emotional pain — close your eyes, take a moment to feel your energy body, and then simply ask to release whatever is not yours: "I ask to release all energies and emotions that are not mine."

Often you will find that making this request of your higher

wisdom will make you feel a great deal better. It is very effective for letting go of whatever you were carrying for others that was not healthy or beneficial for you.

Some may panic a little about doing this exercise: *What if I get rid of something I need? What if getting rid of this emotion will make me lose my friend or lose that person I love because that is one of our connecting points? There is a lot of love there, and I don't want to release that.* Do not worry. You very likely have many connecting points. Besides, we tell people not to go hunting for negative emotions, for they will find you the moment you need them.

For many, the recent years have been difficult. Focusing on joy has taken some effort. The joy is there, but so is the purging and clearing out. You chose to come to Earth at a roller coaster of a time, a time when a mighty group of you elected to move forward together. This movement was already designed before you incarnated. Although we *will* tell you that you are a few years ahead of the plan! Together, you have accelerated your rise to wholeness and freedom. So, despite the darkness, the judgments, the blaming, the cruelty of war, and the many other ways of withholding love that you see around you, this planet is on course for the awakening that was intended at this time.

It is important to know that the acceptance of awakening is stronger than ever. Therefore, the biggest surprise you may get is that people in your life whom you would have written off as "not ready to wake up" have begun to wake up. Or their eyes will pop open in the next year or two. One of the signs of this shift is when you find yourself having a surprising conversation — such as one about emotions, healing, consciousness, or truth — with someone who you did not believe would ever be open to these topics. Keep that in the back of your mind.

But don't let your ego entice you into thinking that you may be one of their greatest teachers. Their greatest teacher will be someone they resonate with and relate to more than they do you. However, a bridge may appear between you — a bridge you thought had burned long ago. The surprising heartfelt conversations and healing that are possible with these people in your life will further release you to be who you are here to be.

YOUR SPIRITUAL FAMILY

You never really let go of anyone. With every single person you appear to let go of, it is not the person you are trying to move away from but the energy between you that is no longer compatible with the trajectory of your growth. You meet many friends and beloveds along the way, each one a gift for your soul's evolution. But the paradox is that the greatest conflicts in your life are with some of your most trusted soul people — your spiritual family.

If you did not trust them so, you would never walk with them into some of those darker spaces and places you have needed to explore. This is the shock. Shock is a big factor when these love relationships that were so wonderful suddenly turn sour and sometimes end abruptly. The shock wave sent through your system is that the energy of love has changed. This can leave you bereft and questioning the love you believed was between you. This change is hard for the human mind to deal with. It will try to come up with all sorts of reasons to help you understand the powerful event that has just rocked your heart.

Feel what you feel in these moments. Drop into your heart. It is the fastest way to reach your answers. The mind will lead you to some understandings and insights, but the *answers* are in your heart — and that is where courage is sourced, too. Have you ever noticed that when you have experienced a sudden and shocking change involving love, your energy renews? And you feel even stronger after a time? You have tapped into your heart energy, where your life force is unimaginably powerful.

At first, you feel weaker and more vulnerable. It seems like love has been removed from your life. But that is not the truth. It is just that the particular experiment and exploration in love that the two of you were cocreating has come to a completion point. *You* knew it would be over. Your mind did not know, but your soul knew.

At these moments, remember to feel. Your feelings will take you very far along your evolutionary path. Many times this is where the ancient wounds are released. Old relationship conflicts resolve, and finally you release the anchor that has made your growth and evolution feel painfully slow at times.

You are the committed one. You have committed to this evolution. So do not be hard on yourself when you feel like you have taken a few steps backward or even hopelessly regressed. If you are experiencing high-low, high-low, high-low fluctuations, recognize that this is a time of great acceleration in your life. In order to go higher, you sometimes choose to quickly dive down into the lower emotions — for understanding, resolution, and occasionally motivation. So, if you wake up one morning feeling uninspired, anxious, worried, or depressed, do not get angry with yourself. Do not judge yourself or entertain the idea that you've done something wrong. You are doing everything right. A part of the journey of evolution is to feel and release those limiting emotions. Feeling and releasing brings you closer to yourself and to others.

Once you have moved through the high-low stage, something more stable begins to arise. It centers around your heart, the foundation of your energy.

THE BEAUTY OF BOUNDARIES

Remember that you have free will when it comes to those people you choose to surround yourself with. If you are around "heavy" people — for example, those who are in a very low or negative energy state for a long time and unwilling to accept your invitation to a higher place — you will find it more beneficial to move away from them than to try to grow through hardship. You will find it more beneficial to set a boundary to protect what you are growing in the garden of your life — emotionally, relationally, creatively, professionally, or spiritually.

This boundary-setting business can be most difficult when it comes to your family connections. Much to others' wonder and awe, some of you have wonderful, open family relationships. Yes, they do exist! But many of you struggle with being yourselves around family members who do not want to see the authentic you. In your minds, this runs counter to the closeness and safe haven that you are told family should provide.

Your openness and love can be difficult for another if they cannot find their way to a similar place of resonance. Your energy can be too much for them before they are ready. So remember to respect the path of development of others. The more you do, the more quickly you will find "your" people. As you let go of some of the old energy templates you carry in relationships, allowing yourself to stop fighting the people whom you want to change or who you wish would finally understand you, you get what Lee rather humorously calls the "upgraded" versions of the people in your life.

This doesn't necessarily mean that people literally disappear from your life, to be replaced by all new faces. What is lovely is that with old friends and new friends, you see that you don't have to fight anyone. Fighting serves only when you finally realize that you are fighting yourself. And many of these "upgrades," if they are new to you, will remind you of friends, family, and lovers past or present, for they will have similar aspects but will be free of some of the conflicts or difficult edges you have experienced in those prior and current relationships.

MOVING FROM JUDGMENT TO HAPPINESS

Judgment of others puts a foot on the brake when what you may really want is to foster trust, closeness, and connection. This applies in the same way if you judge yourself. When you recognize that you are being hard on yourself or another, celebrate that recognition and then release it. Judging doesn't mean that you have failed — not at all. You have simply put up a wall between you and the connection you could enjoy. The more you notice this dynamic, and release it, the faster you will move into the happiness you desire.

Happiness does not look the same for everyone or in every moment. Happiness can be peace. Happiness can be feeling safe. Happiness can be optimism. Happiness can be curiosity and exploration. There is no *one* way. Allow your happiness to expand.

Exercise: Entering into Love's Healing Zone

Take a moment to relax. Take a deep breath in, and breathe out any tension that you may notice in your body.

See if you can feel yourself opening — opening your inner vision, opening your heart.

Bring to mind the people who have come into your awareness as you have been reading these pages. This could include someone you love and adore who is still close to you, someone you loved in the past whom you did not have such a good ending with, or someone in your life now whom you love but are having a difficult time reaching or connecting with. See each of these individuals, however many there are, standing ahead of you in this vision.

Now feel your love for them — even those you have conflict with. To fight with somebody, you really have to love them. You really do. Otherwise you would have no investment in the fight; you would just walk away. Allow any judgments you may have about arguing or fighting to drop away for now.

And now feel the love they have for you. Are there sensations, colors, or sounds associated with these love feelings? Let yourself feel it in your own unique way. And allow yourself to receive their love, individually and collectively.

Remember that even though some people are not so adept at expressing love and other emotions, it does not mean they aren't experiencing them. There are many who think highly of others and feel deeply for them, yet they would not dare express it directly.

Your love is felt. Their love is felt. Breathe into it...sensing that love is what is most enduringly real in your world.

Do not worry if your mind is still viewing one of these people as an enemy. Let your mind think whatever it wants. We are not talking to your mind. We are talking to your heart. And it is the *feeling* that is the most important part in this moment. So feel the love you have for each one of these people — and, again, feel the love they have for you.

Basking in the light of this love, know that you are shedding the energies you need to shed in order to free the parts of you that have felt constricted around some of these individuals in your life.

And when you are ready, allow yourself to release this experience, knowing it is done. The love has worked its healing magic on you — and them.

PUTTING YOUR WHOLE HEART INTO LOVE: THE GREAT ANTIDOTE TO FEAR

The fear of change in relationships is one of the biggest fears you face. You know these fears intimately. Your connection begins with great happiness and hope, yet the fears begin to assert themselves.

The fear of not being good enough.

The fear of being rejected.

The fear of being replaced.

The fear of being "suffocated" by the relationship.

The fear of being bored over time.

The fear of "losing yourself" in the relationship.

The fear of repeating the "mistakes" of your parents or others.

The fear of loss through divorce or a breakup.

The fear of loss through death.

The fear of not knowing how you could possibly survive without this beloved.

The fear of having your heart broken.

Fear, with its many faces, can feel like an insurmountable energy. But oftentimes stepping into your fear is the only way to see that it has no power over you. It may even be working *with* you! For example, if you feel you are in a relationship or friendship that you do not wish to be in any longer, but you cannot figure out why you can't leave it, trust that you *will* leave it if and when you need to. In the meantime, there is something here for you.

You are not a victim, even if you are feeling stuck at this moment. When you look more deeply, you can see that you are choosing to be here in order to learn, discover, grow, and reclaim aspects of yourself. Fear may be holding you in place for a good reason, until you are ready. So, the self-judgment and self-blame that go hand in hand with the idea that you have held yourself back are not true. You are where you are, doing what you are doing, experiencing whom you are experiencing — and you know exactly why.

Looking at all your relationships with this kind of honesty and awareness is one of the ways you can tap into trust. And the way to know that you are tapped into trust is that it brings you closer to yourself and others. It invites emotional vulnerability and builds true safety. Every relationship you have, especially the one with yourself, can be called successful when trust is present and strong.

Exercise: Seeing the Real You

Take a slow, deep breath in. And as you breathe out, feel your connection to your body, your heart, and the inner life that is so active in you.

With a soft gaze, see in your mind's eye a person up ahead. Let them gradually come into focus. This person is *you*. But you look different from how you saw yourself in the mirror this morning. You are more beautiful, more vibrant, more alive, and more awake than you have ever seen yourself.

Is this you in the future? No, this is you now. Let this in. See this true mirror of who you are — with your talents, skills, and abilities; the creativity that you express; the love that you give.

However much you may want to argue the point, you do not see yourself clearly. You hear it said many times, but you do not always take it in. See if you can take in the truth that is obvious to everyone who loves you:

You are extraordinary.

The occurrences in your life that you have deemed mistakes, missteps, or failures do not detract from this truth. They only add to the texture and richness of your being. You are extraordinary. When you walk into a room, you change the energy in ways that only you can.

See and feel the light that emanates from your soul. Feel the unique warmth of *you*.

When you are ready, return from this encounter with yourself with a greater willingness to be seen by others. Recognize that you are sacred mirrors for one another.

Every person longs to be seen, known, and loved by others. Every person wants to matter — to be significant in the hearts and lives of those they share love with. So we will tell you this: The more you connect to your love, the more clearly you will be seen. The more you connect to who you are here to be, the more clearly you will be seen. Yes, some will not be able to see you fully. Trust that. And just be you, unashamedly and gloriously. You came here to experience being you — freely and without apology. The more you give yourself over to the highest heights of that, the more fun you will have. The more joy you will feel. The more beautiful will be your relationships. The more healing you will bring to the world.

The Relationship Affirmation

What makes me a master of relationships is
my courage, vulnerability, and honesty.
When I fear the loss of someone I love, I love them even more.
When I feel distrust of another, I look within
to see where I'm not trusting myself.
When I don't feel good enough to be loved,
I remember that that belief has never been true.
I was made to love and be loved.
And so it is, forevermore.

CHAPTER 10

FAMILY PEACE

B^{*y the time I recorded "Family Peace" at home in Jan-*}
uary 2007, I must have completed around seven hun-
dred private sessions. It had struck me how there was this
constant theme of family relationship issues. For some peo-
ple, certain family relationships can be so negative that they
need to walk away for a time, or forever. This takes courage
and is never easy. For others, being able to stand alongside
people with whom you have been in conflict or had mis-
understandings is one of the great gifts of life. To experi-
ence closeness, tenderness, understanding, and connection
within a relationship you have believed to be beyond repair
is one of the great spiritual triumphs of a human being.
Equally, to simply come to peace with what is in a family
relationship — feeling whole and no longer yearning for it
to be different — is a great achievement of energetic clarity
and acceptance.

If you have had any family difficulties, this channel may
arouse some feelings. The emotional dynamics within your

family may move through you. That is part of the healing
process. If you feel any conflict rising up in you or any chal-
lenging emotion, just go with it. Just observe it. Emotion
is a great teacher, so allow it to show you the areas where
deeper understanding and growth await you. Just sit back
and make yourself comfortable and absorb what you will
from the channel.

Welcome. We are here at your request to address the issue of family relationships. These are integral to your learning. Indeed, the lesson of family runs throughout your entire life as a human, even if you have had little contact with your family beyond childhood. These are the formative energies, the formative relationships — the relationships through which you initially shape your relationship with yourself and the world.

The significance of family relationships, especially for those who would turn their back on family, cannot be overestimated. Indeed, walking away in itself is a great lesson that the family has provided some of you with — the choice to walk a different path from that of your family. That was an intended action, if that is what you chose. It is an action that you knew your chosen family group would allow you to take.

Before you incarnate in human form, you assemble the group of souls whom you need to teach you, those who fit the life lessons you need for your spiritual growth, *particularly in the early developmental stages of life.* In this way, using your vision as a soul, you choose your family members, many of whom you will have had relationships with in prior lifetimes. You see, soul dynamics both replay and shift throughout the lives of a human.

It is often vital to experience friendship with a past-life enemy, just as it can be important to quarrel with one whom you were greatly aligned with in a previous life. It helps you explore the dynamic energies within yourself, which is the essence of what your family provides for you. Your family group allows you to explore the energy within and thereby come to know yourself.

Family is a profound kind of support, for it is a place where oneness can exist for you, even when there is misunderstanding. Now, we speak here of the *energetic* truth of family, a truth that may not be instantly apparent to you when first considering the situation you find yourself in, for you might have disagreements with at least one member of your family.

What you must remember is that a group — and a group energy — has many different characters within it. If you are able to agree with many different characters within a group, you are well-rounded. This is not better than *not* being well-rounded, but it is important for you to notice this in yourself. Your family can teach you a great deal about who you are when you observe your interactions with self-honesty.

Those of you reading these words will have already looked deeply into this part of your life — many of you at a psychological level, many of you at a soul level, some of you at a heart level. But the important thing to know is that, from an energetic perspective, you and your family are *bound*. That is, not "bound" in any negative sense, but you have a group imprint that stays with you for your entire life — an energy imprint you carry with you everywhere you go.

So be aware: if you are one who avoids family members you disagree with or who seeks to escape family altogether, they are nevertheless part of you.

It is important to truly understand this and to feel that truth within you, for it will help you get beyond the idea of separation — the idea of *energetic* separation, for the energy is different from the personality. The personality is the *experience* of the soul energy and an expression of the soul energy, but it is not the actual energy of a soul.

THE ENERGETIC DIVIDE: WHAT TO KNOW WHEN YOU FEEL LIKE AN OUTSIDER

The first thing to realize about freeing yourself from negative family dynamics and past experiences is that you must first surrender to the energetic link between you and your family. That is a powerful surrender. It frees you from a great deal of strife, for you recognize there is nothing to fight, just as there is nothing to fear.

This surrender has nothing to do with resignation, conformity, giving up, or giving your power away to another. Your individuality is not stripped from you by being at peace with the energetic connection you have with your family members, however different they may be from you. And, lightworker, this is important, for you may have put yourself into a family who bears little resemblance to you.

Many of you are of the crossover generation — the generation moving forward at the peak of a very significant progression of human consciousness on Earth. You are also the generation birthing children of light. So this disparity is becoming less apparent, and your families are vital in this process.

If you are a lightworker who experiences difficulty with your family members, it can be helpful to see them as your teachers and your pupils. They are the souls you practice on and with, as it were. This does not mean you are obligated to heal all those around you who appear to be in your family group. But it does mean that you have the opportunity to connect the dots related to your family — to see the themes, patterns, and story lines propelling your soul's growth.

Often for lightworkers, there is not enough sustenance when interacting with nonlightworker family. It can also be draining when a healing is required of you, sought from you, but not reciprocated or directly asked for or even understood in many cases. In those instances, it can be tiring to give, for you are asked to remain energetically open for hours at a time while tiny particles of light are siphoned off, for that is all that will be received. This is far more exhausting than working intensely with one person who is open to receiving your light. This is one of the big difficulties for lightworkers within families where light struggles to be given, received, and allowed.

So know this and be aware of this in order to release the pattern. From both sides, starting with yourself.

Although some of our words do not surprise you, it's possible you have not yet made these words fully conscious. You have not allowed yourself to be liberated. You see, you have the seed of liberation within you. It is just time to bring these ideas and feelings to the surface, and therefore consciously activate your liberation. And this is what you are doing right now.

As you know, the shift in consciousness on Earth is in acceleration mode. And this speed allows you to move beyond experiencing family as a barrier and step more into the deep acceptance of family. For when you accept family, you accept the world — because, in a very real way (and protest as you may), family *is* the world to you.

This is true whether you grew up with your biological parents or an adoptive family, even if it wasn't "adoptive" in the legal sense. Maybe your best friend's family took you into the fold if you had a neglectful or abusive home life. Or perhaps your grandparents brought you up. In one way or another, for better or worse, you each had your families with you when you were children.

ACCEPTING THE PAST

Allow yourself to look back on your childhood. See yourself and how different you were then from who you are now. It is difficult for many of your family members to move and change as fast as you have. They may struggle to see you as who you are in present time. It is not that they want to hold you back. In order to continue to connect with you, they have to freeze-frame time, for they cannot go where you have gone. They do not know the highway. They do not know the territory. They are simply communicating with you as the "you" they once knew.

For many of you, this energetic divide can be particularly challenging with your parents. Siblings, even those who do not follow your path of awareness, are more able to move with the times, for they are freer to receive the energy of now. But they aren't likely to have such a crucial relationship with you, unless you have a particularly close soul bond or the parental bond was not strong.

Parents are invested in the healing their children bring. They need to be. They are aware that children bring the light for them and to them. Parents need this thread and sometimes get very attached to it, and you, as a result. So forgive them, if you haven't already. Just now, allow yourself to open your heart to your parents, however difficult the associated feelings and invasive their energy may sometimes be. Forgive them, if you can, for they are simply trying to reconnect with something they feel they have lost — a piece of you and a piece of themselves. A piece of their learning.

It is important to *allow* this process, in order to be at peace with your family. You are fully capable of having peaceful and fruitful relationships within your family. That is the truth. But many of you are trying too hard, trying to make these relationships something they cannot be. You need to accept who and what your family is, just as you need to accept who you have become — for only from this place of group acceptance can a new relationship be formed.

So…just *allow* the idea that you have changed over time, and welcome the changed you who you have become. Feel no need to hide this from family members who may not have changed with you, for when you are proud of who you have become, without feeling the need to compromise or silence yourself to make family more comfortable, then you allow your family the same growth.

NO NEED TO HIDE YOUR LIGHT

For the most part, we are speaking to those of you who currently struggle with family, even if there was little or no struggle when you were a child. You could find your way — find your route — and you could recognize yourself within your family. But you are grown now. And you are not just grown in age or personality or wisdom. You are grown in terms of *energy*. That is why you can suddenly feel smaller when you return home, for the size of your energy is not always welcomed if it is not understood. Your family members are not used to it, so you "shrink" to accommodate them.

Don't hide your light.

Be who you are. And trust that through being who you are, fully, the sands of time will shift everything accordingly. Time will allow the truth of you to be apparent within your family. You might argue that this would be a struggle, that this would be confrontational to your family. But it is equally confrontational to *not* show them who you are.

We do not suggest that you push your family to see you or to accept who you are. We simply ask you to not hide yourself. This is important for the coming shift. Many of you separate your family from your work — your energetic work, your path as a lightworker. You see the two as different. They are not so different. There is no difference in energy or spiritual significance. There is simply a difference in understanding and levels of awareness.

～ ～ ～

If you are one who wishes to leave your family behind, there is no need. Truly, there is no need.

If you choose to part ways because you have been pushed to the edge, then by all means act accordingly. By all means, go through the experience you need to. That can be a very powerful catalyst for change. But our point to you here is to allow yourself to expand right where you are within your family group.

This expansion need not be an overt, publicized process. It is internal. And within this expansion, do not allow your family to make you feel smaller than you are, just as you would not allow any stranger to do so. But because there is this energetic link between you and your family, it can sometimes be hard to decipher what is theirs and what is yours. For example, in a situation where you feel diminished or disempowered in some way, are they treating you with disrespect? Or are you treating yourself with disrespect?

Their attempts to silence or make smaller the side of you that is expanded (and that probably has been so since you were a child) are acts of bullying. Acts of bullying come in many forms, some subtle and some overt. It depends, in part, on the temperament of the person delivering the bullying. It also depends on how threatened the one receiving the aggression feels and how far they have been pushed.

So, observe these dynamics closely when interacting with your family. Equally, do you bully or knowingly disrespect any of your family members? Allow yourself to be an observer of, rather than solely reacting to, what your family brings to your door. The power of observation allows for some healthy energetic distance, which will support you in remaining grounded and centered in yourself.

Let us do an exercise to dissolve any ill feelings you have toward family members.

Exercise: Dissolving Family Energy Blocks

Allow yourself to feel the energy of your family all around you. Do not see their bodies, their faces, their expressions, but instead see each family member as a ball of energy. If you have only one family member, it will be one ball of energy. If you have twelve, it will be twelve balls of energy. Or you may decide to treat certain people as groups. You may also choose to see your extended family in front of you. Your inner wisdom will tell you what you need to see. Allow your instincts and intuition to guide you as you assemble the energies of your family who are ever so close to you.

Once you have this imagery in place, allow the energies of your primary parent or parents to come to the fore, to be seen as the focus of these groups. Their energies could take any shape, be any color, but notice how they make you feel.

If your parents are there together, see which of them "steps" forward first. Watch the energy you have conjured in your mind to represent this parent. See where and how it affects you in your body. Does it make you nervous? Does it make your stomach uncomfortable? Do you feel any sensations in your chest area or head? You could find that you have noticeable or strong reactions in more than one part of your body. Wherever it is that your body responds, not only is this the place you are most likely to crumble when confronted with this parent, but it also holds much valuable information for your growth.

- For example, if it is your mind, your third-eye area, or any area in your head that feels cramped or conflicted, then this parental energy is a block to your seeing. It does not allow you to expand your vision.
- If it is your heart that reacts to this parental energy in a negative way, a way that does not feel comfortable or expanded, it may indicate that you feel hurt or neglected in some way by this parent.
- If the energy affects your stomach, you struggle with ego issues with this family member. Personality issues. Clashes. You do not enjoy the fight that you have going on with this parent.
- If it is your lower back or your genital area, your base chakra, it is a sexual block that you are experiencing. But we do not necessarily mean the act of sex here. Sexual energy is your vital life force. It is an essential part of what drives your body and your creativity, so in some way your drive is being challenged by this parent.

See how you respond in any of these ways with each family member in turn. And where there is peace or expansion in your body in response to the energy you see in front of you, there is no great mystery: then you know there is a peace, a respect, an ease within this family dynamic.

Going deeper into the exercise now...if you have a family member you are particularly struggling with, see where it is you feel trapped or bound by this person. Is it related to your self-expression or who you feel you have permission to be when you are with them? Do you feel that they are somehow limiting your choices and opportunities in life?

Once you have identified the energetic roadblock, stay with the block, focus on the block, and feel it within you.

And while remaining focused on the energy of the family member in front of you, see the transformation occur right before your eyes. Allow the block to burst, to dissolve, to expand out of you until it becomes invisible. Whichever way you choose, allow it to move out of you...and away from you.

You can do this. It is not an impossible exercise. If you have difficulty with it, acknowledge any frustration and then let it dissipate. Just keep going. If it is too "burning" for you and for your body, give yourself rest time, and return to the exercise when you can. You will find that the more you do it, the more quickly any feelings of constriction will diminish.

That is what we are working on today — releasing you from the habits of limitation, struggling, or suffering as they relate to your family. Even if you are one who has done great inner work related to your family — released yourself, against all odds, from imposing difficulties and dynamics — you will still have residue in these areas. Doing this exercise frees you, empowers you, liberates you. So, take your time, and if you wish to return to it again in the future, do so.

The gift of this exercise is found wherever there is a physical response, for it points out to you where you struggle. It points out to you the place where you are allowing yourself to be energetically interfered with by this member of your family. And you will replay this interference your whole life with people who carry a similar energy signature — but only until you recognize that your capacity to love is far greater than any pain that has been bound up inside the pattern.

So you see, family represents a healing opportunity. It is not that you must be at peace and have healing with your family members before you can be free of the dynamics. It may be that you reach resolution of the dynamics in unexpected ways and through other relationships in your life, such as friends, lovers, colleagues, or even acquaintances.

The next time you make contact with your family members, you will notice a difference in your behavior. You will also notice a difference in your feelings as a result of this exercise. It is but one step in a journey of healing that you must not shy away from.

If you have rejected your family, if you have turned away from them, check to ensure that you haven't swept pieces of the past under the rug. If you feel you were abused, bullied, or disrespected by your family, it is vital that you do this exercise. Understand that this is for you, not for them. It is *you* who is seeking liberation.

COMPASSION FOR ALL:
A DOORWAY TO EMOTIONAL FREEDOM

Once you have achieved your liberation, your family is that much closer to achieving theirs, but that is not the aim here, in this process. The aim here is to further free *you*, for freedom is what you need and deserve. As you move into the coming decades, having clarity and being light and free emotionally will greatly benefit you. There is a great abundance available to you in every part of your life as you become ready and able to open your arms to it — abundance on the physical, emotional, mental, and spiritual planes.

Yes, within you are traces of childhood, the formative years of this incarnation. Those traces of childhood are ready to dissolve now. You will not let go of any positive qualities you gained as a child, but it is time to let go of the mask you put on in order to protect yourself. It is time to change the perception of who you are in the eyes of others. The hardest gaze to bear is often one that comes through the eyes of one (or more) of your family members. But remember that they are innocent, as are you. They are doing what they know best and living in the way they know they can.

They struggle as you do.

THE SWORDSMANSHIP OF BOUNDARY SETTING

At the same time, keep your sword with you at all times — and by "sword," we mean the sword of boundary. To heal and grow, to live and love, boundaries are vital. And they are for you to draw. People will invade your boundaries. People will invade your space. People will attempt to take advantage of you. You can be sure. But this is nothing personal. This is simply life. This is simply humanity when fearful and unconscious.

The way to both remedy and avoid this is to be clear on your own boundaries and your own energy. And when another pushes your boundaries, make them even clearer. This is another aspect of what we mean when we speak of the sword — the sword of truth that all of you are equipped with, even if you haven't used it for years or decades.

There is no greater place to practice the swordsmanship of boundary setting and truth telling than within family.

If you experience difficulty with family (and almost everyone does), you will invariably experience difficulty with others in the world. This dynamic will repeat in you until it is resolved. So why not go directly to the heart of the matter? Energetically, you can do this within yourself at any time. It need not involve a quarrel or a conversation mired in misunderstanding. Your family loves you to the best of their abilities. Sometimes their abilities can be greatly lacking in comparison to yours, but so, too, do they experience you in this way.

It works both ways, remember. If you are a lightworker within a family where lightworkers are not the norm, they experience a loss of you as much as you experience a loss of them.

You experience the loss by having family members who do not have your awareness in certain areas, so you do not feel you are *with* your group. Look at their side of things, also. They are not dealing with a member of their group as they know it, either, so they, too, are trying to reach a halfway line, just as you are.

Giving yourself this time to ponder your family relationships, both in childhood and adulthood, will enlighten you a great deal about your relationship to the world, but most importantly, about your relationship to yourself.

For it is all about you.

What you experience is born of *how* you experience. So trust. Give yourself time. And know that no matter how much you may still need to clear emotions or feelings within yourself that are not who you are, you are already free. You are ultimately free behind these masks that you have been exploring. Know that and feel it in your heart. And release your family members in order to release yourself — in order to experience more of yourself, more of them, and more of life.

Taste the emotional freedom that is yours.

A CLOSING NOTE FROM LEE

The exercise that the Zs outlined is worth repeating. You can do it within your own time and space so that you can reexperience what comes up. Venture into the reactions you have, and then change them. Manipulate that energy within yourself and dissolve it.

Although it can take a few attempts to shift energy, you have already shifted something today. Trust that.

In addition to the focuses of this channel, I want to touch on one other important subject — the throat chakra. This is the area of our communication, so when we are feeling stifled or trapped in communication, it is common to manifest illness or a block of some type in that area. So be aware of what it means to you if this is an area that seems to react to any members of your family. Does your throat tighten? Do you get hoarse? Do you feel a lump in your throat? Does your voice become a whisper or, on the other end of the volume spectrum, become high-pitched?

Is there something you need to express to someone or about someone? What do you need to say? What do you need to put into words?

And the final and most important piece I want to offer you goes back to the topic of freedom.

We are all free.

Our families are also free.

In truth, they are as free from you as you are from them.

If you can come to them with respect, at peace with who they are and who you are, a true meeting of minds can take place. Rather than a fight, conflict, disappointment, blame, or judgment, something surprisingly good can happen.

Last, remember that whenever you approach any energetic work like this, you have to be good to yourself in the days following, because there will be movement. There will be a shift in you, and this may occur in a different way anytime you choose to revisit this chapter. And when you are done with it, you won't revisit it. You will be *done*.

You will be more integrated. More settled in yourself. And more available to love and be loved.

Love and peace to all.

Family Freedom Exercise and Affirmation

Are you currently struggling with a family member? If so, where in your body do you feel the conflict? And what are you in the process of simultaneously releasing and embracing?

Area of body where physical response is felt:	Relates to:
Mind/third eye	Seeing/vision
Throat	Communication/expressing yourself
Heart	Love/relationships
Stomach	Ego/personality
Lower back/base chakra	Sexual energy/creativity/life force

With this awareness of what's happening in your physical body and your emotional body, repeat the following affirmation three or more times:

At all times and in all circumstances, I am safe.
I am loved. I am whole.
I am free to be myself — joyfully autonomous and unique.
I am free to belong — an essential part
of the family I choose.
I am free to love.
I am free to be.
All is well.

CHAPTER 11

THE POWER OF WOMEN

⌇

"*The Power of Women*," which took place at a live seminar I was leading on Mother's Day weekend in 2008, was huge for me. I felt slightly weird as a man delivering a channel that represented women and came through female energies, but I decided to trust the process, and I remember how alive everyone in the room looked afterward. I had not heard these messages from the Zs in this way before, and they seemed to boost the morale of the people who had gathered with me that weekend.

"The Power of Women" is a call to arms. It is an invitation for women to know their inherent strength and to stand up in conscious solidarity, because having more and more women in leadership roles is crucial to balancing much of the masculine energy distortion that is at the root of our collective pain. I am heartened to see a shift taking place around this truth, especially during the past few years of unstoppable social activism.

Welcome. It is a pleasure to be here with you. We are excited to discuss what we are about to discuss. Lee has been a little nervous because whenever we are excited, he never quite knows what's going to happen, but that letting go and trusting is a good thing!

We are here today to speak to you of one topic, and it is a vital one — the power and leadership of women and of the feminine as a fundamental creative energy. The world will come into balance through the leadership of women. It will come back into balance the more the feminine energies are allowed to be, without censorship or limitation. This will also occur as men come to fully understand the divine feminine and reclaim this power for themselves.

The divine feminine has within it everything needed for living. It is the energy of *feeling, being, receptivity, intuition, psychic thought*, and *creation* itself. But there is another feminine power that has not yet been truly honored: the gift of *nurturance*.

To nurture another is not fully understood as the powerful life force that it is, but it truly is. The love you give when you nurture, whether you are male or female, is an expression of the power of the divine feminine. And, of course, that is not to say that masculine energy does not hold love or give love. But allow us to zero in on the meaning of what we are saying.

The womb in a female body is the birthing place, the container in which you were formed biologically. Women are potent creators. They give life to the planet, and the male gives seed to the womb; an egg is fertilized and a baby is produced. So this is a profound relationship between men and women. You cannot divide one from the other, really, but a division is exactly what has happened societally, and for a very long time. As far back as the Bible, the divine feminine has been very cleverly edited out of your narratives. It is now coming to light that females who were prophetic at the time, including those who are celebrated in that great Book, were hidden from view by some who altered the scriptures. This is not news. You have been dealing with the repercussions of this for a long time. Many men have seen women as a great threat, and you are still dealing with a significant measure of what you know as sexism and chauvinism. But let us rename those words and simply call them *fear*.

This is a fear of the feminine principles and energies, especially the capacity to feel and express emotions. And this fear gives rise to resistance and anger, as some people resist the heart opening. There are those individuals who are threatened by what they have inside themselves and what you have inside you, those who would push against you or resist.

This is the predominant experience of women throughout time. This resistance is also what men experience as they increasingly get in touch with their hearts.

At the same time, it is true that the power of a woman can melt a man's heart — inviting openness and vulnerability. Yet many men are not ready to have their hearts touched in this way. If you are a woman, you have tried many times to encourage your men to speak from the heart, to be *in* the heart, and it is always bewildering to you that many of them find it such a struggle.

And then there is the other side of the issue. Masculine power is about will and action, so many women have been disallowed these aspects of their power. For these conflicts to be healed and the divide to be bridged, it is useful to remember that many women have been men in prior lifetimes, and many men have been women. A wheel is turning — a wheel of living, experiencing, growing, and evolving. In a primordial sense, almost all human beings are capable of feeling empathy for the "opposite sex."

THE RISE OF FEMININE LEADERSHIP

If you are a woman who feels great anger about being a female, about being subjugated by men and not allowed your full expression or your power, now it is time to release that anger, for when you deny it, you only lock yourself into that paradigm. It does not do anything to the man you are angry at. It really does not. If he has made a decision to try to control you, suppress you, or limit what he is willing to hear from you, it will not affect him if you get angry. It will affect and limit only you. And the effect is very similar for those men who are in touch with their feminine side. They, too, can experience the internalizing of their anger.

The revolutionary truth for women is that the release of your anger will lead you to your power. And it is safe for you to embrace and express your power now.

Women are moving into more and varied leadership positions in society right now. Many of the greatest leaders on the planet are *mothers*. This is not clearly seen or acknowledged. Yet, mothers know it. It is interesting to note that motherhood is historically the one place — and possibly the only place — where women are given sole authority: the authority of a mother.

It is also important to understand that mothers look to women who are not mothers for inspiration and leadership as well, whether they are aware of that or not. Mothers need those women who are out there doing their work and who have not physically given birth in order to experience the widest-ranging sense of womanhood they can. This, in turn, allows them to be more integrated models of what it is to be a woman for their own children.

As women are increasingly taking on leadership roles in the world, they are changing the standard ways of being in places where men are also in power, and where many of the decisions have unquestioningly been approached in a left-brained way.

Where the logical and linear approach has long been sanctified, there is an opening now to also lead through creativity, connection, intuition, and love.

The feminine is rising. And yes, women are coming forward — and need to come forward.

You may wonder: what does this mean to you personally?

It is time for you as a woman to speak.

It is time for you as a woman to speak your truth.

Just let those words settle in, and feel into what they mean to you.

If you are a woman, it is time to allow your voice. And by the same token, if you are a man, it is time for you to allow your heartfelt, intuitive voice to be heard, and not just by the outer world but also by you yourself.

Where women need to speak outwardly, from their masculine, men need to listen inwardly to their feminine. That is the balance.

A man who chooses to tune in to his feelings and his intuition, and to speak from that inner knowing, will experience what a woman knows. And a woman who chooses to say out loud what she believes and what she stands for, and does so with confidence and without apology, will experience what a man knows.

Now, if you are a woman, you may be thinking, *Yes, I understand the principle, but that doesn't entirely relate to me. I'm strong. I take care of myself.* But at some level all women experience the disempowerment of your feminine energy because of the way society has been skewed — even though you know it is not the truth. And many of you men who are awake and in touch with your feminine energy are quite clear about this syndrome.

But we are stressing this point now to capture your attention: *women are going to be needed in the coming years like they have never before been needed.* It is not to say that men will *not* be needed. And men who are awakened in the feminine, you will be hungrily consumed, also. But women especially are creating the changes the world needs to see. And no matter how long their inner power has been denied, it is time for women to be bolder. This does not refer to the hubris that you judge in certain men you see who are bold with their action. If you are a woman, it is simply time for you to speak from your heart. It is time for you to move through the world without fear or judgment of who you are, because the world needs you. It needs your sensitivity. It needs your care. It needs your innate understanding that when one human being suffers, all suffer.

In your popular culture, some of the most powerful and popular people are women. Consider Oprah Winfrey and the vast influence she has had on your planet. She is one of the first to lead with a balance of masculine and feminine energies in a highly visible and celebrated way in your world. She uses her heart and her intuition, and she uses her ability to choose and act. That is all we are speaking of. The more you unify the part of you that feels, that senses, that knows, with the part of you that is capable and willing to take action, you will achieve the extraordinary.

"What will this take?" you may ask.

First, it will take a little time. There are already beginning to be great shifts in the right direction. And by the time you reach the middle of the twenty-first century, this issue will in many ways be long gone. There will still be some cultures where the women will not be liberated, but you must understand that those cultures are coming to their own understanding of the equality experience. And those who incarnate into those areas of the world are dealing with those issues for themselves, also. It is important to keep perspective and to know who you are and what you have to do. It is wonderful to help others and champion those who are not experiencing the freedom you enjoy, but it is also vital to step forward with what you have to offer the world.

Many of you reading these words are incredibly powerful in your love. Love has been undervalued and underrated for so long. It is not the hearts and flowers emojis that you can find on your phones. It is so much more than that. It is the power of life. It is love that creates human existence. How can that possibly be disputed as the greatest force on Earth? At this time, women are the carriers of uninhibited and resilient love, at a stronger level than men.

Despite the wounds to the energy template of women, you are ready to break out now through your honesty and authenticity, and simply by doing what you wish to do and feeling how you wish to feel.

The power of communication is the tool women will use to change the world — especially the power to communicate feeling. For if you help others find out about their feelings, interpret their feelings, feel comfortable with and express their feelings, the world will change. So much of the violence, anger, and other destructive emotions and behaviors that you would wish to see gone are caused by ignoring and denigrating feeling. Women know this, as do awakened men who are strong in feminine energy. That is why the power of the feminine is needed now more than ever.

GENDER IDENTIFICATION:
WIDENING THE PATH OF EXPLORING

Take a moment to see yourself as the being you are now, and recognize that you were born of the seed of a man and the egg of a woman. You have within you the perfect balance. You may be perceived to be a very "masculine" woman. Wonderful. You may be perceived as a very "feminine" man. Wonderful. Gender identification is becoming increasingly fluid, and the diversity now being seen is necessary. Look to the people on your planet who are transgender, for example. This diversity is coming through to your world in order to balance polarized energies and remove the limitations that the genders have been confined by. If you try to filter yourself through and fit yourself into a tight little pigeonhole of *man* or *woman*, you will forever be limited.

Now, how do you achieve this if those around you are more comfortable with the limited you? For example, if you are a powerful woman who often meets the opposition of powerful men, how do you handle it? How do you overcome the opposition? Answer: You do not engage the opposition. You simply *be* in your truth. Do not bang your head against the closed doors, but keep walking the path you are on.

If you are a woman with projects, visions, and ideas that you have birthed in feminine energy and wish to implement in the world, it is important to understand that you have inside you the strongest "man" you have ever known. You have the ability to drive forward everything you want to drive forward. It is time to take the "bull by the horns" and trust that you can do so while also nurturing and giving and loving. So whether your dreams and goals are simple or grand plans on a global scale, activate them now.

Why the urgency? One of the reasons is because the masculine is in what we would call a *recess* right now, and the masculine actually needs the feminine to grow. Men need women to grow in power so that they, too, can grow in power — authentic, life-affirming power. Their resistance to women is simply their resistance to becoming more powerful. So, men are afraid of the power of women, but they are also waiting for women. At a soul level, men are waiting for women to take more of the lead so that they can see what the next step is — for as women evolve into their power, so will men increasingly become examples of heart-felt action in the world.

This is not to get prescriptive. Every man, every woman is different. Every man and woman has inside them everything they need to reach complete balance and power, and it is only through *balance* that they will achieve power.

The key is simply to open your heart to both sides of your energy.

Exercise: Opening Your Heart to Your Mother and Father

Take a slow, deep breath in, and relax. And again...breathing in ease and peace, breathing out tension and overthinking.

In your mind's eye, look ahead of you and see the two in-dividuals who are your parents. If you did not have one or both birth parents at the beginning of your life, bring in an energy representation of your parents.

See your father on the right-hand side and your mother on the left-hand side. See them however you wish to: You may see them in physical form. You may see them energetically. Trust that whatever comes to you is perfect, sensing that they gave you everything they were capable of and did the best they could when it came to nurturing you and giving of their energy and love.

Now look at your father, on the right, and see who this man was as an expression of the male energy. Was he a masculine man, a feminine man, or a balanced man where energy was concerned? Just notice this part of your energetic heritage. And in your own way, take a moment to thank your father for giving you life. This may be confrontational if you do not have a good relationship with your father, but remember that you're thanking him for giving you life, not necessarily for *raising* you. You're thanking him for being the vessel through which you chose to get your first taste of masculine energy — for however you experience your relationship with your father, there was an alignment energetically otherwise you would not have birthed through his seed of energy.

So take a moment to thank him for this life he gave you, and see who he was. See who he is. See what you came from.

Now shift your attention to the left and see your mother. This is the woman you came through into the outer world. This is the seed of female energy you needed in phys- ical form. She is the woman whose womb was your cra- dle of creation for the nine months leading up to your first breaths. In this moment, simply thank her for giving you life. (There is no need right now to communicate about any of the details of your childhood.)

You came here with many aspects of yourself (skills, talents, gifts, capacities, challenges, lessons to be learned) not sourced from your birth parents. You are entirely your own soul, but your first doorway to Earth was through these two people. It is important to see and acknowledge that truth, and then find the place in your heart where you can authen- tically thank them. If you had — or still have — a difficult relationship with one or both of your parents, it is especially vital to thank them for giving you life so that you can finally let go of identifying with them as limiting factors with re- spect to who you are now. When you have thanked both your parents, just allow them to disappear into the mist.

Now take one more breath, and release this exercise.

SETTING YOUR PARENTS FREE

By doing the preceding internal exercise, you are being the spiritual parents to yourself. You are consciously representing the masculine and the feminine, the male and the female, the mother and the father. These are the primary energies that drive your life.

Many human beings have a more challenging relationship with one of these aspects of self than the other. If you are strongly identified with one particular parent, it can often be that you are stronger in that form of expression and way of being. You may be more adept at expressing the feminine, motherly, nurturing side of yourself. Or you may be stronger in the masculine side of yourself and your ability to provide for and protect those in your care. Humanity has evolved, and there is no longer a preset role that you need to adhere to. You can color outside the lines now and allow your feminine and masculine energies to be expressed and shared in *your* way.

And one of the most potent ways to do so is to free yourself from believing that your mother or father did not give you what you needed. They gave you life. They gave you the seeds of feminine and masculine energies from which to grow. And so, to look back for too long at how they failed you is to miss the point of what you are capable of. You were supposed to go beyond them — and you are succeeding.

ACCESSING AND OWNING YOUR SEXUAL ENERGY

The physical act of sex between men and women is a powerful example of the *energy relationship* between male and female. Where a male can give his energy to the woman through this act, she receives whatever is inside him and it catalyzes her. A woman has a great ability to receive his energy and transmute it in innumerable ways. Both people are giving and receiving, giving and receiving. This physical representation is but a primordial example of that back-and-forth dance of energies.

If you are a woman who feels that you are not so good at receiving, then this is the only area you need to look at, for you already have the male side down. If you can allow yourself to just focus on receiving, and receiving alone, right now, you will be surprised by how extraordinarily your life will change.

Paradoxically, women over the millennia have become good at receiving intense emotions, such as anger, from a man in the joining of energies through sex. Although it's not a conscious receiving of energy, women often internalize the anger of men due to their depth of empathy and receptivity. In this instance, however, we are talking about anger in a more expansive way.

In anger, there often lies power — and we're not referring to power that is aggressive or destructive, not at all. It is often by channeling anger that a man's love and sexual energy can be tapped into and expressed. It's a part of the base energy of a man that drives him forward. The importance of remembering this now is that it is time for conscious women to find the fire in your own belly, with or without the male energy exchange. It is also important for men to allow themselves to be as intuitive and as open as the women they admire the most.

To both women and men, we say, recognize that you do not need to access your innate power through one another in unconscious ways. You have it all inside you. Women have for so long been catalyzed by men, and have waited to be catalyzed by men, but that is changing. And it must. Because women will change the world.

To the women reading these pages: *You* will change the world. Men will join you, but women everywhere are greatly needed now — with all your gifts that give rise to cooperative and courageous leadership.

FREEDOM FROM COMPETITION

One of the keys to embodying and accelerating your power as women is to heal the wound of competition. It is often the case that women are fighting other women, and this is a tragedy. Women are competing with other women for what they see as limited positions of power, for it appears that men are given *their* places of power and women have to take what is left. This fight is destructive, and it does not help or serve you at all. It only slows you down.

If you are a woman and you find yourself in competition with another woman, look within and see for yourself whether there may be a part of your heart that is not accepting your own feminine power. You may, in fact, be in judgment of feminine power. Do not be hard on yourself if you see this; it is just a societal program that has been running for a long time, and you can be free of it. The girls on your planet right now want to be free of this program, too. Instead, they want to be nurtured by your leadership as women. And so, to become free of the shackles of competition among yourselves is one of the most profound gifts you can offer to all those looking to you for direction and inspiration.

In the coming times, as women you will have no choice but to take your power. And awakened men will have no choice but to surrender to the feminine. That is the path of evolution at this time. You will bring balance to the world, and you will feel compelled to give of your particular gifts. Be it through the nurture of your child, the work you do, the creativity you express, the leadership you provide to other women, or the leadership you offer men, your unique ability to bring balance and unity will prevail.

There will be some men who will resist it, but they will just be resisting the feminine power inside themselves. They will just be resisting their own love. When you are in these situations with men, draw on your inner masculine. Stand strong in communicating your truth and your feelings. Your courage and resilience will create a ripple effect of great positive change for both men and other women.

The power of women is inescapable, anyway. Feminine energy is hitting the planet now in waves of a magnitude you cannot imagine. Feminine energy is sponsoring the opening of the heart and the opening of the power of love. And love has the capacity to transform any negative energy.

HEALING THE WORLD WITH FEMININE ENERGY

Take a moment now to feel and connect with the feminine energy inside you. Whether you are male or female, agree to open to your feminine energy and power. You can do this in words, if you wish, or just by feeling your inner agreement.

Your feminine power is the missing piece for so many of you, and the truth is that it is right here, just waiting for you to claim it. It is not that you have refused it; you simply have not collected what is sitting there, as it were, just waiting for you. You need only embrace it.

What will reclaiming your feminine power do?

It will increase your level of feeling.

It will increase your intuition.

It will increase your vision and the possibilities for a brilliant future.

But most importantly, it will increase your *aliveness*. You will get very busy with this energy. More and more, your *doing* energy (masculine energy) will be informed and directed by your own depth of feeling, intuiting, caring, loving, and *being*. And that is an amazing aspect of your feminine power. Action inspired by feeling is creating new systems, new organizations, new infrastructures, and new rules in your world today. And there is so much more innovation coming — innovation led by the feminine, and by women.

You are one of the influencers of this new time. Understand that.

You can affect one person, and through that person thousands more, as each one spreads what you have given them around the world. One of the ways you deeply affect people is when you are honest with others about what you feel, without censorship — even when you are speaking to those you fear would not understand or would reject what you are saying.

If you have an impulse to speak, speak. People, including men, will be compelled to listen. Just ask to open to this feminine power of yours and enjoy the renewed sense of energy that comes into your life.

And do not be afraid of being exposed to more of the anger, pain, and violence in the world. The more you understand, celebrate, and give of your feminine energy, the less of this anger, pain, and violence there will be on your planet.

All will be well. All *is* well.

The Feminine Energy Affirmation

I open to the feminine energy inside me,
and I am ready to discover new dimensions
of this sacred creative force.
It is safe to embrace and express my feelings.
It is safe to abide in my sensitivities as an intuitive, empathic,
and nurturing human being.

CHAPTER 12

RADICAL EXPRESSION

The Doorway to Transformation

I n August 2015, I gave a talk to a large audience in London *at an event called Energy Tune-Up. People came from Wales, Italy, France, Germany, and beyond, making for a really vibrant evening. My parents and some of my oldest friends were also there, which was special for me personally. The venue was energetically lit up before our group even walked through the doors that night. The London Festival Orchestra had been practicing a beautiful symphony in that very space earlier that afternoon and was still playing when my team and I arrived.*

With any event I do, I never know exactly what I'm going to talk about until the group is assembled. It quickly became clear to me that this audience of lovely people was representative of the larger world — a world where a tremendous amount of energy is being uncorked, an incredible amount of vital life force unleashed. Self-expression is the outward-flowing manifestation of this energy. We're witnessing this expression every day with the voices of individuals,

*groups, countries, races, gender identities, and others grow-
ing louder, clearer, and stronger.*

*So what is radical expression? As you will discover in
the following pages, it's far more than a neat turn of phrase.
Personally and collectively, it's a quality of communication
that is a catalyst for change while simultaneously giving us
the strength to meet those changes. It's our courage made
manifest, whether through our words, our actions, or simply our vibration. It's radical because it activates our full
power and influences the way we move in the world.*

*Whether spoken or unspoken, it is communication so
real, honest, and true to who we are that it transforms the
landscape of our lives.*

*I think it's precisely because change shakes us to our
core that this intuitive talk came through in a fiery and
sometimes humorous way. I hope that the pages to follow,
which comprise the only chapter in the book (other than the
introduction, "When Destiny Calls") written directly in my
voice rather than as channeled guidance, will inspire you at
the deepest level.*

I have worked as an energy intuitive and a channeler for a long
time now. For more than a decade, I've been tracking the energy of
people, places, and events — sensing, translating, and giving voice
to what is going on within and between us, and usually beneath
the surface of our day-to-day experience. Not surprisingly, I
see certain themes come up over and over again. Two of the most
burning areas of focus are relationships and personal boundaries — which, of course, are intimately connected. Another
major focus has to do with how we move in and through our
lives — often concentrating on work, life purpose, and what we're
contributing to the world.

One of the common denominators among these major life themes is *expression*. Expressing ourselves is so much more than putting into words what we think and feel (although doing that is profoundly important). When we express ourselves, we are communicating who we are, what we need, what matters to us, what we love, and more. We are asserting and affirming — through our relationships, our work, our actions, our feelings, and, yes, our words — that we are *here*.

We are in this world and a part of it.

We are a part of each other.

And it is through our expression — and what we *choose* to express — that we are directly creating our reality.

There is a quality of expression that has less to do with what is on our minds than what is in our souls. That is the expression I'm calling "radical," because it asks big things of us. It asks us to know ourselves and to be deeply honest about the state of things — where we are in our lives, what's working and what isn't working, and what we need and want. It requires honesty, first with ourselves, to find our way out of unhealthy situations and destructive patterns and into solutions that are empowering.

Back in the nineties, psychologist Brad Blanton wrote the book *Radical Honesty*; he was a harbinger of where we are today, both in the world and in our own lives. We're in a time of radical honesty, and it's not always comfortable. It's not easy to suddenly learn the truth about something that you thought was other than it is. It's not comfortable to confront a mask you've worn most of your life as a form of protection. It's not comfortable to tell the truth, to yourself or to another, about a way of being or behaving that doesn't work anymore. The way I put it to myself is that it's not always comfortable to own my own bullshit. But I prefer to catch it — the story, the self-deception, and so forth — as it's happening, for the purpose of becoming more aware. Once I become aware of the need for change, I can take the necessary steps toward implementing that change. It's not enough to acknowledge only the wonderful things in my life, the aspects that are high-functioning and fulfilling.

For me, having grown up in England, one of the cultural ironies is the incredible richness of *artistic* expression (think Shakespeare or the Beatles or Monty Python) alongside the stifling of *personal* expression. Of course, we can find that same paradox in any culture in the world. Expression runs in parallel to repression and suppression.

THE FEAR OF SPEAKING OUR TRUTH

It often feels quite emotionally risky to be honest with another person, and sometimes it *is* risky. We can be so afraid of sparking conflict with other people and risking varying degrees of separation and loss that we bury the truth inside ourselves. We keep quiet. Or we feel one thing and say we feel something else. These distortions actually cause great destruction to both ourselves and each other.

Fear of expression is a dominating force. To break it down into very simple terms, it is the fear of expressing what you feel, think, need, or want. It's the fear of fully expressing who you are and who you want to be in the world. And the fear usually creeps in and takes charge in an incredibly subtle and gradual way, beginning in childhood — in the first instances where we were trying to emotionally survive whatever difficult situation we found ourselves in. Some people grew up in tough homes, where a struggle for emotional and sometimes physical survival was the norm. Others of us grew up in more supportive environments.

Either way, the subtle energies and dynamics that foster the fear of expression find their way to us.

Do you remember time on the playground? Things may have been relatively calm at home, but what happened during some of your formative experiences at school and in other social settings? There were those moments on the playground, on the sports field, or at camp when we started to compare ourselves and compete with each other, moving on to judging and rejecting each other. That's when we start to pull self-expression back in and dial it down. By the time we grow into adulthood, we've developed an unbelievably creative set of strategies for managing what we express and what we do not.

Underneath all this is the fear of rejection or disconnection from others.

The Story of Jill

Here's an example. Let's say your name is Jill, and you and I have been good friends for a long time. But a niggling problem has developed. Every time we see each other, after we greet each other with a hug, you tousle my hair. You run both your hands through my hair and enthusiastically turn me into a rumpled mess. Internally, this upsets me. You always smile and let out a squeal as you tousle away, as if it's an act of total affection, which only intensifies the mixed emotions that swell due to having my boundaries crossed by someone I know and care about. As you're leaving, I say, "Well, it was lovely to see you, Jill," waving goodbye before I run to a mirror to make sure my hair is in order again.

And this goes on for a long time.

Can you think of a situation in your life where you're in a relationship dynamic that keeps repeating? At first, it bothers you only a bit. Then it morphs from light frustration into full-blown anger. And eventually, it hurts you.

If you're Jill and I challenge you on your behavior, you might say, "Oh, don't be ridiculous. You're just so adorable — come to think of it, I used to do that to my little brother when we were growing up."

Without attacking you, I could respond in a firm way, saying, "This is my body, Jill, and I don't want you to mess with my hair anymore. And that isn't negotiable. The head is a very vulnerable part of a person, and it feels incredibly invasive, especially because it has happened repeatedly. If it keeps happening, I just won't be able to see you. That's the line I'm drawing."

You, as Jill, nod in agreement (even though you're not really listening), and off you go.

Or you say, "Sorry, Lee. I thought you liked it. You've always laughed when I do it." And you do it again.

And although I can hardly believe that you did it again, I find myself trying to quell my feelings and justify your actions in my own mind: *Hmm, maybe I am making more of this than I need to. Maybe I'm being overly sensitive. I should just ease up a bit and see what happens.*

Whatever day you come around next time, your hands are in my hair again within seconds, despite my previous admonishment, and suddenly I'm a disheveled mess. I have a knot in my stomach and can't deny that it feels oddly abusive. I say, "Okay then, Jill, this doesn't work for me. I can't spend time with you right now."

If you are Jill, my enforcing that boundary with you is going to have some kind of impact on you. It may serve as a wake-up call for you to change your behavior, or you might get genuinely upset with me because you're not used to being given a boundary. You could be on the verge of an emotional explosion anyway — and perhaps that's what I'm most nervous about. I'm most concerned about how you will react.

~~~ ~~~ ~~~

This is the very moment when a lot of conscious people — those who are quite empathic and sensitive — go wrong, because they're often trying to "save" or manage everyone around them. *But how is Jill going to feel? Is my boundary going to upset her?*

The Other Side of the Story

Put yourself in my position now and imagine that Jill is your friend.

Jill is messing up your hair and dragging her knuckles against your head every time she sees you — and you really don't like it! Yet you override yourself each time. *I don't want to upset her. She had a terrible childhood.* Yes, true, but we all know people who had terrible childhoods who will leave our hair alone.

We're so afraid of upset and conflict. We limit our own expression due to fear-based beliefs whose origins we often don't remember — for example, because of what happened on the playground. We told off that kid on the playground and he cried, and we felt guilty and sad. Or *we* were the kid who cried.

I used to have the "save-everyone syndrome." And then years ago, a dear friend and mentor said to me, "Upset happens and people get annoyed at you. And you know, relationships change and people don't always stay friends." I remember that as a really important and empowering moment for me. Before then, I would push my own thoughts and feelings down and sometimes tip-toe around people who seemed unpredictable or volatile in some way. But in doing that, I did them and me a disservice.

This is how suppression leads to resentment.

Maybe I would have truly served Jill years earlier, the very first time she tousled me, if I had said, "Jill, I don't like that," and had a conversation with her immediately rather than suppressing my feelings. *But I can't upset Jill! And besides, she's essentially kind and loving, so I'll just put up with this little annoyance.*

But here is the problem: putting up with little annoyances and not communicating how we really feel rarely works out well. Little annoyances can grow into gnawing resentments. Our outer layer, the edge of our energy, takes the hit the first time. But then with every repeat offense, the hit gets deeper. In it comes, in it comes, in it comes, until the deepest part of us has been affected. Eventually, we find ourselves saying, "Ugh, Jill is coming around, and I wish she wasn't."

Or we say, "Well, Jill should be different!"

Nah, Jill is Jill. Jill is absolutely going to be who Jill is.

The real issue is: are we not being who we really are when we are with Jill?

BOUNDARIES: AN ENTRY POINT TO PROFOUND FREEDOM

No matter how long the pattern has been going on, are we willing to be honest with Jill now?

You could say to Jill, "You and I still have a chance for a transformation. But I'm done with this pattern in our friendship. It's costing me. I've lived with it for five years now. I apologize that I didn't say something sooner. But now I need it to change."

Either Jill is going to get deeply upset, and that will be a catalyst for her to change her behavior; or she's going to get upset, and I won't see her again. Or perhaps she will hear me out and come to understand what I'm asking and why. Whichever way it goes, drawing the boundary line is going to be a positive change in my life. The feeling of freedom that I will have in my body in that moment of cutting the dynamic is profound.

A mechanism within us works hard to keep everything in control, seeking safety and harmony. And while safety and harmony are important, if we opt for a semblance of them at the expense of authenticity, there is a massive buildup of repressed energy. And then, boy, we are bound to see the lids coming off, causing all sorts of upheaval.

On the other side of it, there is something really exciting about taking the lid off in a conscious, authentic, and compassionate way. For example, with Jill, I could zoom out from all the anger and hurt, and look deeper. *Okay, I've had at least seven Jills in my life, seven versions of this dynamic, over the past ten years. Maybe I could have learned to express myself to Jill #5 or #6 ... because poor Jill #7! She got all the exasperation and resentment that had built up over the previous six!*

Jill #7 represents all the people who show up in our lives to unmask and shine a bright light on areas of continued disempowerment and unresolved pain. She is the composite of so many of our girlfriends, boyfriends, spouses, bosses, colleagues, and close relatives, as well as other sacred messengers who have come to bring us home to ourselves.

Do you have a Jill #7 in your life right now? If so, what is that person trying to get you to say or do by engaging in a particular dynamic with you?

WHEN THE HOUSE COMES DOWN: LETTING GO, COMING ALIVE

In the self-development world, change is a hot topic — the importance of change, the need to change, how to change, the secret to changing. But the truth is that as much as we long for it and chase after it, we're also really afraid of change.

We can look in almost any direction and see the death grip

on doing "business as usual," a clinging to the status quo. In just about every country, culture, government, organization, and community right now the structures we have relied on for safety and security are rattling and shaking more perilously than ever before. And, of course, what we're seeing in the outer world is also going on at the center of us individually.

Kundalini energy is being awakened internally.

Life force is on the move, and we *feel* it.

We are being asked to deeply let go of that which no longer serves us.

But often we are afraid of letting go. We're afraid to let go of the relationship, the job, the address, the belief, the attitude, the behavior. Like with Jill, we're even afraid to let go of a relationship dynamic we know is unsustainable, one that usually becomes painful as hell if continuously avoided. We are afraid to tell the naked truth about something that really matters to us for fear that the whole house will come down.

Well, the house *is* going to come down — and several times in life.

The house comes down.

The house gets rebuilt.

That's transformation.

And there is another layer of fear to address. We're not *only* afraid about the house coming down. We're also nervous about the new space left in the aftermath of that change, and what we will do with it.

For example, if I have been playing this Jill dynamic out with seven different people at various points in my life, I've grown seriously used to that behavior. And there will now be personality traits in me and ways of being that I have built around those connections — which have become more of a construct than an actual relationship.

Beneath the surface, we get nervous that if we change the unhealthy aspect of a relationship, the entire thing will fall apart. But it doesn't fall apart, really. The relationship just becomes something new.

This level of truth telling and living in a more awake way sets off a chain reaction. When we get used to speaking the truth in one area of life, we begin to experience that energy of honesty in another area — and then another. We begin to get this *feeling*. It's the enlivening feeling that suffuses us when we come to the end of the road with a particular conflict that we've been in for a long time. We finally utter the words "I can't do this anymore. I've had enough." And we walk away. It's not easy, and we have a kaleidoscope of feelings about it and about how the other person may feel. But at the same time, we can't help but notice the life force that is rushing back into us, lifting our sails to the wind.

Oh my God, my energy just came back. I feel alive again.

BECOMING A MASTER OF BEING YOURSELF

The time we are in right now is incredible on a metaphysical level. The speed with which the insights, understandings, and changes are occurring is unprecedented. The firing off of new awareness and clarity is happening at a shocking pace.

With all this velocity, you can get really good at stepping out of old patterns. You can become a master of developing and ingraining self-awareness and self-honesty. *Yeah, I'm a bit depressed today. But I'm generally less depressed than I was last year, so there is progress.*

I've traveled extensively over the past few years, and wherever I go I notice a new depth of expression around emotions and being human. There is more vulnerability, tenderness, and compassion — and that is what we all want so badly.

INTUITION: YOUR SOUL SIGNALS

Our destiny is being reframed and reshaped every day depending on how we show up: The truths we tell. The choices we make. The willingness to grow and change.

Destiny says, "Okay, we'll give her this new boyfriend to help her get over the boyfriend she was with a year ago."

You start to date that new guy, but then you meet someone else, too — someone who is a lot more like your old boyfriend.

So this is the choice point. You're offered an upgrade boyfriend or the old pattern.

This time, you choose the old pattern. You choose what is your habit.

Now, even though it's not going so well with the old pattern in a new form, it's familiar. In a little bit of time, either you get to the point where you say, "You know what? I've already done this relationship dynamic before. Thank you. You're very nice, but this is not for me." Or your resolve crumbles and you go back into your comfort zone.

Six months later, you're looking sickly and have run out of energy. You're turning up at events holding the hand of the more predictable boyfriend, and your friends are nervous to say anything to you (kind of like you were with Jill). Your last boyfriend was a bit tricky, and they don't want to get in the middle of that again. Meanwhile, you're just going down, down, down, inside your own soul. Stuck in the habit.

It doesn't have to go that way. Your destiny path is constantly signaling you through your intuition. The beauty of intuition is that it's like a GPS installed by your soul — constantly rerouting and rewiring you based on your choices. It's calibrating you to more and more courage and honesty. It's leading you to greater empowerment and freedom of being and expression.

Of course, following your intuition doesn't mean that every wish is going to come true, that every situation is going to work out the way you first envision it, or that the path will be clear of all obstacles. *Well, I had this intuition that I was going to be Joe Smith's girlfriend.* So what happens inside you when being with Joe Smith isn't what plays out for you? Do you decide that your intuition isn't trustworthy? Do you mistreat yourself in some way? Or are you kind to yourself around the disappointments and hurts that you sometimes feel? Do you recognize that the situation has changed, and so, too, can you?

We get attached to various pathways, destinations, and outcomes. And we forget that the only attachment our soul has is to our growth. All it wants to know is: are we growing and expanding? Our soul doesn't say, "Yes, she needs to marry that woman named Yvonne, and it will all be great! Gay marriage is on the way, so that will work out well. They're going to have a house in Birmingham, and they're going to have three kids." No. The soul is overseeing the deeper undercurrents of transformation, less focused on the specifics. "She needs to experience empowered love without restriction."

Destiny says:

We put Yvonne there for her, and she didn't pick Yvonne. And while there was a possibility that she would stay with Yvonne, she walked away from Yvonne after a month because she was not quite ready for that depth of love. She chose the next one in line so she could see how painful her relationships can be when her choices aren't aligned with her innermost being, and she stayed with that person for six months until she got sick.

We are constantly redirecting and being redirected. And learning to tune our dial to the frequency of our intuition makes for a more fun-filled journey...no matter how many twists and turns there are along the way.

I have taken a somewhat awkward path toward my own intuition. I wasn't one of those intuitive wonder kids; I just knew I was hearing and seeing things that seemed out of the ordinary. I was actually a master of suppression until I was about nineteen years old, apart from my creativity. Creatively, I was a firebrand. But in terms of intuition and my sensitivity, I was brilliant at stuffing it down in a variety of ways, and primarily through compulsive eating, bulimia, and being very overweight. I went through difficult experiences that kept me closed until my opening began at seventeen years old. Over the next several years, my personal search and the numerous shifts I experienced resulted in an immediate, quick access to my intuition and my ability to channel.

That was more than twenty years ago. Intuition is at an all-time high among us today, but we often make the mistake of thinking it's more complicated than it is. I can't tell you how often people (including friends, clients, and people who come to my events) will tell me, "Wow, I got this intuitive hit, and it feels significant, but it can't be right because it was too easy." We think there must be a mystical key to unlocking this ability. Some of us secretly hope to find out that we actually do have the magical powers we pretended to have as a child. But it's usually not like that.

One of the turning points for me, which has allowed me to

completely trust my intuition, came when I recognized that my intuitive abilities are coming from a higher source that is cleverer than I am. That source helps me see my own limitations and human blind spots as much as it helps other people work through theirs. It took me a long time to acknowledge this and to acclimate to it because I've had the same conditioning as everyone else. In our culture, we're told, "No, that can't be right."

If you look at some of the earliest writings on intuition and channeling, they often come in the form of religious teachings. This has been problematic due to the sin-and-punishment model of religion and how that separates people from their own immediate and personal connection to spirit. At the other end of the spectrum, there are people who think that intuitive abilities and communicating with other levels of consciousness is just too far "out-there" and simply beyond belief. However, my work with people over many years points to an invisible symmetry that is happening before actual logical events occur. With all that I've studied, explored, and experienced, I'm prone to believe that so much of what we walk into in our lives is planned out for us. Not every aspect, not every detail. We have free will. But there is that destiny path that is alive and well and calling us toward our greatest selves and reconfiguring us for more soul growth and love.

Where in your life would you like to express and share more of your unique strengths, skills, talents, and gifts? In other words, how would you most like to express your greatness?

One of the brilliant things about your greatest self is that it is fully capable of handling and holding the changes that you may have been trying to keep at bay.

As you express your true self, your greatest self, you serve everyone you love in the highest way, especially in those times when they're feeling fragile or lost or afraid. None of us are meant to do it all ourselves. Sometimes we can't find the answer or solution on our own. Sometimes we can't find the way out of the hole by ourselves. Sometimes we need each other.

In that sense, fully expressing yourself in the way we have been exploring here is a pathway into *leadership* — into being the leader of your own life. Radical expression will have you taking the lead toward honesty and vulnerability, ready to make changes in your life when your growth depends on it, and trusting that you will know how to ride the waves of transformation that come of that.

TUNING IN TO YOUR INTUITION

If you would like to test-drive your intuition right now, think back to our conversation about Jill. Did any people, places, situations, or events come to mind as you were reading about our little hands-in-hair drama? That information is coming from your intuition. That's it. It's that unglamorous and that simple. It is just you reading your own internal map.

Your intuition arises daily. It's that sense of something that causes a tingling or goose bumps. It's you knowing that your friend was going to call, or you thinking of someone and a few hours later their email shows up in your inbox. It's that moment when you decide to drive down a street you don't usually take and unknowingly avoid the massive pothole you would have encountered on the accustomed route. These are ordinary examples of the psychic "information highways" that are getting quicker all the time, signaling us at lightning speed.

What signals have you been receiving lately?

Writing Exercise for Transformation: Radical Expression in Action

Expression is a directional energy that absolutely changes what happens in front of you depending on what you are expressing and to whom. And expression becomes super-charged — radically effective — when it comes from a place of personal alignment. When the real needs of your body, mind, heart, and soul are taken into account, your expression has the power to move mountains. And this alignment isn't as hard to achieve as most of us think.

Yes, it can be scary, and sometimes even a little terrifying, to be emotionally vulnerable. But when you take a slow, deep breath, and then allow your next sentence or action step or choice to be deeply honest — congruent with who you really are and who you are becoming — the strength and courage you need in that moment will be right there. They will rush to your side.

In a very real way, accessing and exercising your own personal kind of radical expression is your magic. It's the answer to being the Harry Potter of your own life story. So how would you like to put your magic to use at this moment in your life? What do you need and want to express right now? Dropping below the surface of things, what do you find there? What truths do you want to express?

Take out a piece of paper or open up your notebook and write down everything that comes to you. What truths have you been sitting on that you know are percolating below? No need to censor yourself. Just breathe, feel, and write.

Your Truths — Taking Inventory with Compassion

Do they have to do with your body and health?

Is it something about your primary relationship, your love life?

Is there something about your work or professional life that wants to be expressed?

Do you have an old pattern erupting that is causing you distress or pain, perhaps having to do with your finances, your living situation or environment, a close family relationship or a friendship, or something else that is strongly affecting you?

Is there a bruise to your heart that you need to resolve by talking about it with a person you trust or writing a letter to someone?

Is there a creative passion that you want to express in some way?

What about Your Future Self?

Is there a vision taking shape within you that you want to express?

A dream you want to bring to life?

A project you would like to start?

A collaboration you would love to pursue?

A contribution you are burning to make?

Taking Action — Start with Just One Thing

If you could change *one thing* today, what would that be? Is it a circumstance or issue that feels huge, almost insurmountable? Or is it something relatively small but which you know would be satisfying to shift? Is it an improvement or upgrade to some area of your life? And what can be done immediately in that direction? Just hold an image of that change in your mind and write it down.

This potential is only in your awareness because it is possible for you to change it. I promise you: you wouldn't be able to see it if it wasn't possible. That doesn't necessarily mean you can change it in twenty-four hours, but you can bet that it will change quickly if you refrain from disempowering and degrading yourself with judgmental self-talk.

SPECIAL NOTE ON MAKING CHANGES
DURING CHALLENGING TIMES

I understand that some circumstances are very difficult to shift — for example, if you're a caregiver for a loved one and you want to make changes to that situation. One of the best first steps I know of is to ask yourself: *Where is the oxygen?*

Oxygen is the word I use for the people I love who, when they walk into the room, increase the oxygen. I can really breathe with this person. I can be unbridled in my expression without worry that I'm going to offend. I can be myself. And the more I can be myself, the clearer I am about the decisions and next steps that invite my greatness — and the more others are able to breathe freely in *my* presence.

Who and what provide more oxygen for you?

CHAPTER 13

THE ANGEL BEHIND YOU

❦

*"*T*he Angel Behind You" is adapted from a recorded session with the Zs at a recent Energy Mastery retreat in Norway. I chose this as the closing chapter of* Energy Speaks *because of the spiritual power of its message — that you and I are never separate from the divine. We are never separate from a loving and clear presence that is looking out for us as we navigate the complexities of human life. The pages that follow will put you in touch with this presence — with your inner observer angel, the subtle awareness that towers above the noise of life, holding you close with its unfathomable compassion and wisdom.*

Some of the most beautiful letters I have received are from people who have listened to the audio version of "The Angel Behind You." My hope is that the written version will find its way to your heart in similar fashion.

Welcome, masters! You are at the beginning of a golden time, and in the early stages of the dissolution of the old ways of inhabiting your beautiful world. You are watching as everything around you is shaken and sometimes crumbles, and it is not always easy for you.

Across the whole of the universe, the depth of emotion that human beings hold is what characterizes you as unique.

The many levels of emotion and compassionate consciousness you are capable of reaching are only beginning to be understood. Added to that, the human heart and mind gravitate toward safety and security. Therefore, to experience what is perceived as your survival structures being rattled — and sometimes disappearing — is difficult, for as human beings you are feeling beings.

For the most part, your planet is inhabited by very peaceful, loving people. At least 90 percent of you want openness, acceptance, sharing, and collaboration. You want to love one another. That is the central desire even if the way to achieve it is not always understood. And that desire will grow as the years go on.

But the smallest percentage of your world — a slice inhabited by individuals who are in positions of economic and political power but are usually hidden from public view — actually like war and keep it going for reasons too complex to include here.

Those who want peace rather than war are affected on a daily basis by a world that is continuously broadcasting these conflict energies. You have only to turn on your television for five minutes and flip through the channels to see images and hear rhetoric that are aggressive and violent, what we would call *antilife*. These intrusive energies are being transmitted into the minds and energy fields of human beings at an unconscious level.

As easy as it is to point a finger "out there," at those who do not seem to care about the world, perhaps the most sobering realization is the amount of cruelty and suffering endured within the privacy of the human mind. When you notice judgmental thoughts toward yourself or others, you are dealing with conflict energy. You are dealing with the internalized energy of war.

Those who are proud of their ability to never attack others are often the ones who are worst afflicted with self-judgment and self-criticism — *because the energy has to go somewhere until it is fully released.* When a person has learned to never be outwardly combative, the dagger turns inward.

Now is the time to alleviate — and to end — the secret suffering. And the solution is so much closer than you think.

MEETING YOUR INNER OBSERVER

Anytime you find yourself in a struggle — such as feeling bad about yourself, getting stuck in a painful behavior pattern, or arguing with a loved one — in truth, you are standing at the door of opportunity. It is a chance to become the master of your own energy. We invite you to take the struggle as a signal to immediately stop and confer with the part of you that calmly witnesses the movement of your life — the *observer* part of you.

Begin to feel the presence of the observer. It is not to the left or the right of you. It is not out in front of you. Your observer is the part of you that sits along your spine, directly behind your physical body.

As a compassionate, loving witness, your inner observer is also one of your angels. Through its kind eyes, you can see yourself with a beautiful clarity. Use this clarity to look within: *Am I judging myself? Am I attacking myself? Some part of me is completely identified with what is going on in the outer world, and I am turning it into conflict within myself. Instead, I will recognize this energy and hand it over to my inner observer angel.*

One of two things will typically happen when you do this: (1) The energy will dissipate because you have sent it in a different direction in your energy field, one that has a lot more space or room. Or (2) you will be quite happy to practice "handing over" your conflicts, because each time you do, it strengthens your relationship with the part of you that can simply observe what is going on without getting embroiled in problem-solving.

What we are giving you is one of the most empowering healing techniques we know of — an energetic way to neutralize conflict inside yourself (especially when directed *toward* yourself) by developing a relationship with your inner observer angel.

ᕬᔟ ᕬᔟ ᕬᔟ

Your inner observer angel, to use the popular term, "has your back." It can dissipate any inner conflict or act of self-violence as soon as you hand those energies over. At the physical and energetic levels, you must first allow the conflict to leave your heart and stomach areas. Let us explain.

Many of you are striving for deeper connection with one another. And if you are not striving for deeper connection, it could be that you are feeling depressed or temporarily shut down, for connection is what makes you feel *alive*. When you feel a disconnection from someone, whether for just a moment or for a prolonged period, it is your heart that experiences emotions such as disappointment, sadness, loneliness, and grief. When it comes to your stomach, you may feel the impact in a way that is hard to ignore. You may feel "kicked in the gut" by life events or gripped by fear or loss.

Take a breath into your stomach area right now. What do you observe as you do that?

Giving attention to your heart and stomach centers begins to immediately dissipate the heavier energies that can weigh you down.

Earlier, we equated self-judgment and inner conflict with internal violence. Sometimes the recognition of this violence toward self can trigger feelings of shame. There is no judgment here with us, but judgment is so hardwired inside the human being that when a window of light is offered in order to reveal such inner dynamics, some people can feel worse before they feel better. The judgmental self can kick in even harder. And the shame can intensify for a while.

Shame is a very effective way to keep yourself small, sequestered away from life. And while there are a great many myths and misconceptions on your planet, shame is one of the greatest lies of all. Shame creates a separation between the person who feels ashamed and just about everyone and everything in their world. Toxic shame is the idea that not only have you done something wrong but who you *are* is wrong.

So, if you don't like hearing or seeing the word *shame*, if it sends a shiver down your spine, then good! Let's be done with it.

Allow your inner observer angel to take the shame. Let it unburden you.

THE BREATHTAKING MAJESTY OF YOUR ANGEL

The angel behind you is one of the most powerful forces you will ever know. You see, this angel is built like a Spartan warrior. It is completely gender balanced — "gender irrelevant," we would like to call it. Male-female, masculine-feminine, in the perfect symmetry.

One of the reasons your angel is situated behind you is because if you were able to turn around and see it, you would fall over upon witnessing its enormity and grandeur.

Depending on your physical height, your angel can be anywhere from eight to twelve feet tall. It is broad shouldered, with huge wings capable of dissipating dense energies in a second.

Is that connected to me? Is that part of me?

Yes, and yes.

The truth of its existence would be a shock to the part of you that has played small and found comfort in being invisible.

But the truth is that you have behind you an enormous, loving beast of an angel, so strong that it can neutralize your internal war in the blink of an eye. It is not to be mistaken for an "earth angel," as you like to call them, those humans who do incredible acts of selfless love. This energetic angel, both within and surrounding you, is something different.

It is a fire of uncompromising truth and of profound peace.

When you finally do turn around and see this loving warrior angel behind you that you are an essential part of, you will either laugh or cry to realize that you didn't know this about yourself until now. And while we always recommend laughter, tears are sometimes necessary to fully release the energy of unexpressed emotions.

Just remember to laugh at the end of your tears and you will be in good shape.

COMMUNICATING WITH THE ANGEL BEHIND YOU

The angelic realm is always available to help you, but you have to remember to ask. You may have heard this before, and it is true. If you are bold enough to ask, the help and support will come swiftly. It may take a day; it may take a week; it may take a second. But it will come.

When it comes to your human companions, sometimes you have to ask for help from them as well, as they can't always be tuned in to your needs. However, there are touching moments with loved ones — husbands, wives, girlfriends, boyfriends, mothers, fathers, siblings, dear friends, cherished colleagues — when you *don't* need to ask. There is an understanding between you that, as much as possible, you will help each other. You will look out for each other and do for each other.

At all times, your inner observer angel is there for you in this way, too.

An important distinction to understand is that you are not asking your angel to *take* your troubles. You are *giving* them to your angel. As an ever-present, always-loving part of you, it does not feel separate from you. It wants to lighten your load. It sees your happiness as its happiness, and vice versa.

Therefore, let the conflict of self-judgment, the conflict of self-doubt, the conflict of self-blame, the conflict of shame arise in you so that you can give them back to your inner angel.

And we do mean "back"...to the angel that stands behind you.

OPENING YOUR HEART TO HOPE AND POSSIBILITY

Are you in the midst of difficult days? If you are, know this: As you are reading these pages, you are remembering and strengthening the connection between you and your inner observer angel — a connection that has always been. Your awareness of this relationship is awakened and will get stronger.

If you have felt stuck, battling conflict patterns or painful beliefs about yourself, embrace hope now. Know that your energy field is highly changeable. When it seems like you have run out of all human answers or solutions, that is the time to turn to the etheric body, *the etheric knowledge*. This is where new possibilities lie in wait for you.

If you are struggling on a certain day, it sometimes helps to remember: *Ah! I am having a human day. Everything will be okay.*

Your soul is very present with you on difficult human days, when you are going through a lot of growth...and growing pains. Recognizing your humanity and its density on such days can be very freeing to your entire energy field — when the soul observer, your etheric angel, has been invited to share the experience with you.

⚓ ⚓ ⚓

We understand that the word *density* doesn't sit well with everyone. It seems contrary to the light of consciousness that is such a big focus and quest for many. But think of it this way: When you are cleaning your home, you are aware of the dirt you're removing as you freshen your space. You look straight at it. "Yep, there's the dust and grime. There's the built-up dirt." You just go straight for it. So, when you're addressing your emotions, thoughts, and perceptions in order to freshen your *inner* space, see if you can approach the "buildup" — the density — in a similar way.

We understand that it can be frustrating and sometimes hard to do this, because some of the density is actual suffering. But we also assure you that it is much easier to change your environment once you are not pushing against it...and that brings us right back to where we began....

You are at the beginning of the golden time for Earth, but you are also in a dissolution time. The golden time for Earth is one of living with far more consciousness than ever before, but a struggle is occurring right now around supremacy: who is going to be in charge?

Destructive desires are being driven forward by a small number of beings on this planet. And life-affirming desires are being driven forward by an enormous number of beings on this planet. So while the percentages favor those who are open and loving, this time period on Earth is not easy for you or for the individuals around you.

But remember, you are here as a consciousness leader. As you continue to go through your own emotional journey, you are opening your eyes more and more to the intricacies of what is taking place. This takes courage and is looked upon with reverence by spirit. And while it is true that knowledge is power, what is even truer is that *self*-knowledge is power. You need to be able to look within and know which areas to "clean up" and how to best meet your needs within your current environment.

It is not selfish if you are choosing to work strongly within the realm of energy and consciousness during this time of transition. It is not wrong if you choose not to be at the local protest. You have decided that you are going to clear the conflict energy within yourself.

Likewise, it is not wrong of the protesters to protest, to fill *that* need. It is just as important as what you are doing.

In other words, each unfolding role and focus is perfect.

The reason why it is a struggle for some of you to believe that everything outside you is perfect and everyone is perfectly playing their part is because that would mean that you must also be perfect and perfectly playing your part. And even for a few of the most advanced among you, there is still a level of internal violence that will not let you see things that way . . . and that, too, is perfect.

All you have to do is recognize that this is the game you are playing with yourself. You had forgotten that you have an inner observer angel who will bail the dirty water out of your boat every time you point and shout, "Dirty water on board!" All you have to do is monitor the water.

Some of you get anxious at the idea of giving the bailing task to your angel because you have become such hard workers over the years and don't want to be retired from your duties. *Who will I be if I'm not busy fixing stuff?*

While it might be a little scary at first, as you begin to ask for and receive help from your inner observer angel, you may experience a wild progression of feelings. If you feel some confusion or bewilderment at first, it is likely to be followed by an opening of your heart and a surging of your creative fire that will forever change your life.

With that, let's do a visualization where you can contact the angel within you.

Visualization: Wrapped in Angel Wings

Breathe deeply into your belly.

Whether you are a woman or a man, understand that you are pregnant right now, metaphorically speaking. The creator in you is always pregnant. You are birthing something new, someone new within yourself. It is important now to protect and look after yourself the way you would if you knew you were carrying a precious new life in the womb of your being.

Ask your inner observer angel, who stands steadfastly behind you, to wrap its wings around you.

Breathe in...and out.

Feel the wings as they softly brush against your shoulders and arms, crisscrossing the front of your body.

Sense the warmth of their shimmer as they reach to protect you — forming an energy shield over your solar plexus and heart, your third and fourth chakras.

Feel the profoundly tender strength that envelops you now. And breathe in...and out.

If you would like, ask your angel to cover your entire torso and head, cocooning you within its stillness — quiet and calm and radiantly alive. Its enormous wings can easily hold you without constricting you in any way.

Breathe in...and out.

Be assured that your angel *knows* you. Whether you are a mother, father, teacher, healer, caregiver, leader, or lover of the world (or combine many roles), it knows how much you give, how hard you work, how driven you are to make a difference. It knows of your heartbreaks and your dreams.

It knows you are here for a purpose.

It knows the fire in your soul.

It is aware of all the energy required to be you.

If it would be healing to do so, let yourself feel tired for a moment — unapologetically so. Let yourself fully drain of energy. Just as you are the angel to so many others in your life, allow yourself to be the exhausted one right now, while you are shielded and protected by glorious angelic wings. These wings will recharge you very fast when you surrender and drop into them.

Breathe in...and out.

Let yourself drop down a little deeper, resting more completely inside this sacred cocoon.

Now allow yourself to sense the regeneration taking place while you relax in this space — feeling peaceful, tender, helped, supported, soothed. Feel the rejuvenation coursing through every cell in your body and every part of your energy field — clearing and "fluffing" up your energy on every level of your being.

Breathe in…and out.

In words, images, or energy alone, let the angel behind you feel the gratitude you would like to share with it before leaving its amazing embrace.

The protection coming from the angel behind you is not about shielding you from villains, lions, and tigers. As your observer awareness, it can protect you when your energy becomes low or depleted. It can protect your emotional body when conflict energies arise. It can protect your heart when fear or pain comes. Your job is to pay attention to your needs and to step back into the wings of your angel anytime you need to.

When you do, you will be surprised by the levels of nurturance and empowerment you will feel. You will be astounded by how strong you will become internally and externally.

Initially, make an agreement with yourself to work with this meditative process for a period that feels best to you. Is it three days, seven days, or ten days? Once you begin, your angel offers you an air lock of sorts, providing easy passage between your physical self and your etheric self. As you adjust to being with your etheric self, you will not want to leave. It may feel foreign to you at first, but we would recommend at least five minutes with your angel as often as you wish each day.

YOUR PLACE OF PEACE AND REFUGE

The angel behind you is the guardian of your silent awareness — your inner home. This will be one of the safest places to be in the coming few decades as the earth goes through many changes. As human beings, you are not immune to the hyper-doing and hyper-externalization of your world.

We are not implying that the externalized world will not be safe, but we are affirming that coming back to the voice and touch of your soul will always keep you centered and clear. It will show you the course corrections that will occasionally be needed. It will confirm the road map that is right for you to follow.

Long ago, you agreed to be here on Earth on the condition that you would be able to bring more of this soul energy to your fellow human beings and to the planet. And you are doing that. When you occasionally run out of juice (that is, energy, inspiration, passion, clarity, direction, or humor) from all the doing, wrap yourself in the wings of the magnificent angel behind you and return home to your spiritual power.

Held in the Light Affirmation

The angel behind me is the guardian and amplifier
of my expanded awareness.
It lovingly witnesses all that I experience
and knows the depth of my heart and soul.
Held gently in its wings of light, I am safe.
I am clear. I am awake. I am home.

CLOSING

YOU ARE LOVE

———⟨⟐⟩———

You are clear. You are ready.
There is nothing in the past in the way of your future.
There is nothing in your future that will be anything like your past.
You are clear. You are ready.

This path you've been walking has taken you in many directions.
You have experienced feelings that you did not expect to feel.
Feelings of love, feelings of grief, feelings of anger, feelings of joy.
The full spectrum has been experienced.

And here you are in the center of that spectrum.
At any moment you can move into any one of those feelings.
At any moment you can experience those feelings with or
through another being,
a crowd, a group, or just yourself.

Because you are everything. You are the world.

Your biggest job here on Earth is to love yourself
and to learn to love yourself,
especially when you feel unlovable.

And that won't always be easy.
Sometimes that will be very, very challenging.
But many times, that journey will be very, very wonderful.

And with that goal as your focus,
everything else will fall into place.
Greater opening, greater compassion, greater passion,
greater desire to be here.
The desire to *be*.

When you learn to nurture and love yourself as you would
       another,
when you give yourself that attention,
things change very fast.
Things move in you.

The joy of touch you can receive from another
becomes self-touch.
You can hold yourself and feel held in so many ways
when you apply self-love to your life.

Love is who you are; it is the essence of you.
Love is who you are; it is the essence of you.

Breathe that in.

And again, breathe in the love that you are.
It is ever present, and sometimes
it is just to the right of your shoulder.

On the days when you feel you cannot find it, it is always only
    inches away from you, waiting, watching, encircling you.

While you go about the busyness of undoing
whatever it is you are undoing.
What have you just been undoing in yourself
these past days or weeks?
Have you been undoing grief?
Have you been undoing depression?
Have you been undoing a tangled relationship?
Have you been undoing self-criticism?
You will know you've been trying to undo these things because
they will have taken all your focus.

When these emotions or energies come to you,
they are asking you to see them.
They are asking you to free them.
You can free everything.
You can free yourself.
You can love yourself.
You are free to do this.
You are free to love yourself.
Even if you feel you are in the most confined prison.
Even if you feel there is not love around you.

These are the most important times to practice self-love.

Because everything is vibrational.
And all the vibrational frequencies that you exist in and around
    every day,
and those you hold within yourself, are like magnets to others,
jigsaw pieces, sometimes.

So when you and your frequency sync up to self-love,
    then you can be sure that even more love is coming.
But the beauty of self-love is that when love comes to you,
you do not need to hold it, to fear it, to believe it is the key.
You will simply recognize love sent your way as a mirror.
You will know that you are holding that love for another and
    sending it back.

Love is the gold of the earth.
There is so much to love on the planet.
There is so much to love about people.
There is so much to love about yourself.
And you have barely come close.
And this self-love has nothing to do with ego; it has nothing to
    do with a perception of why you should be loved or whether
    you deserve to be loved.

This self-love is a pure remembrance that everything is love.
There is no division — there is no division from source.
Any perceived division is illusion.
You are everything.
And when you remember this,
anything and everything is possible.
Everything and anything is possible.

So breathe. Fill your belly.
Stroke your belly as you breathe.
Love this part of your body, this part of yourself.
Caress it, hold it, fill it with breath.

You have no idea how lovable you are. It's incredible.
You are so very lovable and so very loved.

You are loved by nature. You are nurtured by it.
It gives you everything you need. For all your senses.

So, if you are ready to awaken to greater love, repeat this aloud:

I am everything in creation
I am pure love in the human body
I am here to share, expand, and grow
I am love, and love will always find me
I welcome love with open arms
I welcome love with open arms
I welcome myself with open arms

Breathe.

You are clear.

You are love.

ACKNOWLEDGMENTS

It takes a village to deliver a book to the world, and so many great hearts showed up for delivering mine, which makes me deeply grateful. Thank you to all who were involved:

My editor and soul sister, Debra Evans, without your sensitivity to channeling, to words, and to me, this book wouldn't be what it is.

Marc Allen, Kristen Cashman, Georgia Hughes, Kim Corbin, and all at New World Library, for believing in this book and giving it a home that feels so aligned energetically. I am so happy you are the custodians of this work, and thank you for all you have all done to support it.

Amy Hughes, my literary agent, you rock in every way!

Tracy Cunningham, for the wonderful cover; and Regina Meredith, for the gift of your friendship and the deep wisdom of your foreword.

The whole team at LeeHarrisEnergy.com: Noah Perabo, Marti Bradley, Anna Harris, Amanda Douge, Patty Sherry, Rebecca Hall, Nick DeLa Cruz, Meghan Svetich, Davor Božič, and Narada Wise.

Anna Harris, Marti Bradley, Claudia Brazil, and David Brand, for the transcription and editing work of the early editions of some of these chapters.

The early Limitlessness.com period of my work: Story Waters, Claudia Brazil, and Joshua Van Abrahams.

All the attendees in the workshop rooms across the world where these channels were first verbally delivered and birthed. And to all those readers of the early editions of *Energy Speaks* who championed the words and energy here: I heard you, and you inspired me to create this ultimate new edition.

A special thanks to my parents, Meryl and David Harris, and the rest of my family, for your ongoing love and support of me and what I do in the world. And to my husband, Steven Washington, for being the love and the home I return to every day, along with our furry companions, O and B.

Last but never least, thank you to the Zs for trying to get my attention and managing to do so. You and this work have changed my life for the better. I salute you, and I love you.

LEE HARRIS ENERGY RESOURCES

⌔

Lee Harris Energy offers an exciting and ever-expanding collection of tools and events for transformation. Focusing on topics such as relationships, intimacy, emotions, health and healing, abundance, money, self-empowerment, self-love, sexuality, meditation, being an empath, finding your purpose, and many other core aspects of life, Lee Harris Energy online includes the following key access points:

EVENTS — In-person retreats, workshops,
and trainings, and online courses
www.LeeHarrisEnergy.com/p/events

THE STORE — Audio programs and music albums
at the evolutionary edge
www.LeeHarrisEnergy.com/store

THE PORTAL — Lee's Conscious Community

www.LeeHarrisEnergy.com/p/the-portal

VIDEOS — Monthly "Energy Updates," healing wisdom,
instruction for empaths, and more

www.LeeHarrisEnergy.com/p/videos

ABOUT THE AUTHOR

Lee Harris is a gifted energy intuitive and channeler who leads a vibrant online community that reaches over one hundred thousand people around the planet every month. His acclaimed Energy Mastery retreats and Energy Tune-Up seminars are adventures into the deepest aspects of living, loving, and awakening.

Lee is the founder of Lee Harris Energy (LHE), the company that supports the production of all his events and products. In addition to authoring *Energy Speaks*, Lee is the producer of more than one hundred transformational audio and video recordings.

An accomplished singer-songwriter, Lee has been writing and producing music since 1998, collaborating with musicians in Europe, the United States, and beyond. In 2001, he debuted his first album, *Shapeshifting*, followed by the albums *Phoenix* and *Golden World*. His most recent release, *Arise*, was cowritten and produced with acclaimed Slovenian musician and composer Davor Božič. Lee has recently begun his sound-healing work with the *Adventures in Sound* series.